Book Savvy

CYNTHIA LEE KATONA

THE SCARECROW PRESS, INC.
Lanham, Maryland • Toronto • Oxford
2005

SCARECROW PRESS, INC.

Published in the United States of America
by Scarecrow Press, Inc.
A wholly owned subsidary of
The Rowman & Littlefield Publishing Group, Inc.
4501 Forbes Boulevard, Suite 200, Lanham, Maryland 20706
www.scarecrowpress.com

PO Box 317
Oxford
OX2 9RU, UK

British Library Cataloguing in Publication Information Available

Library of Congress Cataloging-in-Publication Data

Katona, Cynthia Lee, 1947–
  Book savvy / Cynthia Lee Katona.
    p. cm.
  Includes bibliographical references.
  ISBN 0-8108-5434-1 (pbk. : alk. paper)
  1. Books and reading. 2. Reading. 3. Best books. 4. Books and reading—
United States. I. Title.

Z1003.K38 2005
028'.9—dc22

                                                          2005000562

∞™ The paper used in this publication meets the minimum requirements of
American National Standard for Information Sciences—Permanence of Paper for
Printed Library Materials, ANSI/NISO Z39.48-1992.

Dedicated to
Tish Whitcraft

The man who doesn't read good books has no advantage over the man who can't read them.

Mark Twain

CONTENTS

I

WHY BE BOOK SAVVY?

1

AUTOBIOGRAPHY
OF A BOOK JUNKIE

No one is a born reader; sometimes it just looks that way. We all expect the pert little girl who grows up in a perfectly civilized household—surrounded by colorful and enticing books, with parents who read to her every night before she goes to sleep and lovingly organize regular outings to the library (capped off with a stop at the ice cream store)—to grow up to be an avid reader. But the remarkable thing is that lots and lots of children who don't grow up in such nurturing and cultured environments still grow up to love books and reading, sometimes acquiring the passion a bit later in life, and sometimes in the most unusual of ways.

I am a good example of a book addict who grew up in a home that some folks would call "deprived," who didn't get her first "hit" of fiction until she was fourteen and wasn't thoroughly "hooked" on books until long after she graduated from college. My story is proof positive that book addiction can happen to anyone, anytime. Of course, I hope that you have already "got the habit" and that you are already seriously "addicted," but if you're not already "under the influence" I would love to be your "connection" to the world of books. Think of me as your friendly neighborhood book "pusher."

I grew up in the 1950s, before the era of politically correct language, as what people used to call "poor white trash." Back then, lots of kids growing up in inner-city Los Angeles could answer to that *sobriquet*. I came by the title honestly, being the "illegitimate" child of a waitress and a gambling man (civil weddings having no cachet in the Catholic Church, as the nuns continually reminded me). I had uncles who would drive all the way from LA to Georgia on long weekends just to bring back a little real moonshine, and who thought there was nothing more glorious than finding a good bit of road kill, fresh enough to barbecue in Griffith Park. I was half-Sicilian and one-sixteenth Sioux, and I didn't know enough to check off the "Caucasian" box on official forms until I was a teenager.

I hasten to add that I was not an unhappy child—quite the opposite. My world was full of colorful distractions: Hollywood back in the 1950s and early 1960s was really Hollywood, swarming with big screen immortals. On my many youthful excursions to the Boulevard of "Stars," I was as likely at Schwab's Drugstore to run into Moses (or Charlton Heston, as some people called him then) as I was likely to see an aging Tarzan (Johnny Weissmuller). I ate my lunches at the Hollywood Cemetery sitting on the bench/monument of Tyrone Power, and I could bike to the Capitol Records Building on Vine, go into a booth, and listen to the latest 45 rpm. NBC on Fairfax was a great place to go in the afternoon and cadge tickets to be in the audience in of one of the many live kid shows, like *Howdy Doody*. At ten, I was yo-yo champion of Los Angeles; I had a half-page photo of myself "walking the dog" in the *Los Angeles Herald*. My philandering father had taught me to play a mean game of blackjack, and my mom waitressed at DuPar's in Farmer's Market, where I could always depend on the gals to sneak me an ice cream sundae. Muscle Beach was just a bus ride away, and the summers were hot. Believe me, there was plenty for a latchkey kid to do. But reading definitely wasn't in the mix. I do not, in fact, remember ever seeing a single book in any of my various apartments or halfway houses, not even the *de rigueur* King James Bible.

Thank goodness, the nuns of Immaculate Heart taught me to read, entirely against my will, around 1957. I had no idea what the skill might be good for, but I was sure that it was easier to learn to read than to brook the wrath of Sister St. Francis Cabrini. The nuns' attitude toward books was rather daunting, though. Books were objects of extreme personal hygiene; the nuns were more concerned that books had no bumped corners or folded pages than they were with whether students were enjoying them or not. When it came to books, the nuns gave me an exaggerated respect for the physical object but no understanding or love for what was contained inside. Books became, for me, simply another occasion of sin (cleanliness and godliness being definitely intertwined), not conveyors of joy, or leisure, or happiness, or any other pleasant thing. And yet somehow, by the time I graduated from eighth grade I could read. The nuns, God bless them, had taught me to read, and read well, and read phonetically. I was technically literate, and for this I will be forever grateful.

So at fourteen, I was able to read but unable to figure out why I should bother. I was not, thankfully, without glimmerings of imagination, though. My long-gone biological father, a first-generation Sicilian, who had been functionally illiterate in both his native language and in English, had not been stupid, however, or without a sense of drama and a flair for the fantastic. So while I did not grow up with the classic stories like E. B. White's *Charlotte's Web* or Dr. Seuss's *Sneetches*, I did grow up with incredible, and sometimes morbid, stories of my father's own devising. Every night before I went to bed I would ask him what I should dream about, and his answers were something that would no doubt have made the Brother's Grimm quite content.

I also had the movies. My best friend's older brother was an usher at the Pantages Theatre, and I saw every major movie released from 1956 to 1962, sometimes many times. I can't even count the number of times I watched *West Side Story* and cried till I was weak, or saw *House on Haunted Hill* and marveled over the skeleton that dangled over the audience's heads.

However, when I was fourteen my life was forever changed, and I could not have become more desperately miserable. My mother remarried; I suddenly got a twelve-year-old stepbrother; my beloved dog and all my precious belongings were left behind; my new "family" moved to the incredibly retro, one-theater suburb of Castro Valley, in northern California; I was thrown unceremoniously into public schools; and everything I knew as real life was pretty much over. Little did I know then that this new life would be the making of me.

When high school started the following fall, I discovered, much to my surprise, that I was two years ahead of the kids in public school; my teachers thought I was smart. My Cs and Ds were suddenly coming up As, and I found that I kinda liked not sitting in the "dumb row." At home, when I locked myself up angrily day after day in my room, my amazing stepfather, who was trying valiantly to get me out of my deeply flamboyant teenage depression, started to give me best-sellers to read. It was totally inappropriate stuff for a virginal Catholic innocent like myself—Nevil Shute's potboiler *On the Beach,* Kyle Onstott's slave-trade novel *Mandingo,* and John O'Hara's seductive *Butterfield Eight.* Goodness, how I enjoyed reading them, although I certainly wouldn't let my stepdad know. Hmmm . . . books were sexy, and my stepdad was sorta cool. I wasn't really sure what I could do with that information.

And then I was put in Advanced Placement English at Castro Valley High, where I had the most inspiring teachers. I imagine many people can trace some of the good things in their lives to a caring teacher, and I'm no exception. I remember particularly Mr. Rankin; he was a short, mesomorphic sort of fellow, a wrestling coach as well as an aesthete. He encouraged us—in fact, he required us—to mark in our books, which was extremely painful to me after all the teachings of the nuns. I still have my copy of *1984,* which I read and discussed with much delight in his class, and I am amazed at what a thin, faint line I could make with a ruler and a pencil back then. It can barely be seen today, and I doubt it was much more apparent at the time. Mr. Rankin taught me to "savage" the physical book but to love the characters, ideas, and words contained within.

There was also the remarkable Ms. Butler, who chose me to be Juliet in the school production of *Romeo and Juliet,* mostly because of my great Roman nose, but partly because she was trying to teach me to love litera-ture in the form of drama. Having seen *West Side Story* innumerable times, I was totally prepared for the role.

The lack of things to do in my adopted hometown, my new "smart" friends, and the guidance of my stepdad and my teachers were slowly chang-ing me. So, when I was almost sixteen, it seemed natural that I take a good-paying part-time job at the Alameda County Library as a page (a book shelver). It is difficult now to credit the quiet, reverential attitude toward books in American libraries in the early 1960s. It was the nuns all over again. So for the next seven years I worked my way through school and up through the library system, by taking the oddest jobs available there. I rode on the bookmobile, taking books to the folks in low-security prisons, juvenile-delinquent holding tanks, and county hospitals. I eventually became a patient librarian at Fairmont Hospital, one of the last residential hospitals in Cali-fornia. There I donned a mask to take books to the TB ward, ran reading groups for drug addicts, and read stories to the quadriplegics coming back, in alarmingly large numbers, from the Vietnam War. My life was full of books, but not necessarily full of reading. I knew that Shakespeare was shelved in the Dewey Decimal 800s, but I had still read only one of his plays.

Between my stepdad and my teachers, college was a given. So off I went to California State University at Hayward—the first person, not to mention the first woman, in my entire family ever to graduate from high school, let alone go on to college. Not being born to academia, I signed up as a poly sci major, because it had the shortest registration lines. I was still not "hooked" on books, and I didn't become an English major until my senior year, and only then because that was the major with the fewest re-quired units. I had a rather pragmatic view about getting a degree and get-ting out of college as quickly as possible.

Once again, amazing teachers made all the difference. In my senior year of college I had to scurry to get all my English credits finished, and in the process I found my intellectual home. Mr. Bevin introduced me to Blake's *Songs of Innocence and of Experience,* Professor Rosenbaum gave me back the Bible as literature, Ms. Standiforth showed me the detective nature of research, and Professor Markos guided me so tenderly and expeditiously through my master's thesis that I had my master's degree in a mere two years. I graduated long before I was really ready to leave, but I had learned one incredibly important thing from college—that my real education was just beginning. I was hooked on books, and thirty years later still have an ongoing and expensive habit. (If you're going to mark your books . . . you have to buy them.)

As you can see, never did a more unlikely soul become a professor of English. And like any late convert to a powerful religion, I am the most rabid practitioner of all, proselytizing my life away, trying to get others to join my sect, and unhappy until I can convince every single human on earth to be a reader. Hence the book you have in your hands—*Book Savvy.*

2

INTRODUCTION TO THE
STATE OF READING IN AMERICA

THE MEANING OF LITERACY IN A CULTURE

In 1950, Helen Haines wrote in *Living with Books,* "Today the American public as a whole is potentially a reading public. Illiteracy exists, but in a limited and steadily diminishing degree." As an astute teacher of librarians, she could say something like this with assurance. But what a difference a few decades have made.

Since Haines's era, an abandonment of phonics by well-meaning but misguided elementary school teachers; a truly historic influx of non–English speaking students into American classrooms; a slackening of standards, in all things, since the 1960s; a lack of support for adequate budgets for public education; "white flight" to private educational institutions; and a disproportionate emphasis on "self esteem" as opposed to "accomplishment" in American schools have all coalesced to create a reading crisis in America—the world's most financially and politically developed nation. It is astonishing but true that the rate of illiteracy is significantly higher in the United States than in countries like Costa Rica and Turkey (where incidentally, most people speak English as well as their native languages).

How did this happen, and what does illiteracy mean in a complicated democracy like the United States? Consider Fred, a native speaker, a nice young fellow, whose pleasant manners and affable nature made him a real favorite with his elementary school teachers, teachers who were having to deal with an increasing number of emotionally and academically difficult students. In his sweet and plodding way, he managed to get passing grades in elementary school, and he continued, like many of his peers, to be promoted beyond his level of competence.

In high school, he was reading at a fourth-grade level, but by working extra hard and being quite a good athlete, he managed to slide through with a gentleman's C. So far, so good. The only problem is that Fred had basically wasted twelve precious years of his life in a failed educational environment, and he was being turned out into the world as a high school graduate but a functional illiterate. Yes, he could read, to an extent, but not surprisingly, he was often confused and frustrated by the written word.

Fred only dimly understood what had happened to him, and he tried to go to his local community college to repair the damage, but he could no longer get by with a willingness to work hard and a pleasant disposition. He could now barely read at the sixth-grade level, and academic texts were simply beyond him. Even with the help of a tutor and the total support of his teachers, Fred could not succeed at genuine, college-level work.

So Fred turned optimistically to the world of work, where he discovered that even the simplest job required a considerable amount of literacy. He was regularly flummoxed by job applications. He appeared to prospective employers to be totally ignorant (which was not really true), because he could neither spell nor write a coherent sentence. He was headed, at best, for a McJob.

On a personal level, Fred felt terribly ashamed. He knew that he was basically smart and that he had a great deal of potential, but each year that he got older, it was harder and harder to imagine asking for the help he needed. After all, what kind of thirty-year-old man can't read? He was tremendously sorry that he couldn't read bedtime stories to his own beautiful children; he feared that because of him they would never learn to read either; he was humiliated that he couldn't fill out his own personal tax forms; he hated having to struggle with the instructions for assembling a simple barbecue; and he found maps so confusing that he had difficulty even finding the nearest unemployment office. Computers and the Internet were wonders that he watched passively on television. In fact, Fred watched a lot of television. He tried to keep up with current events. He was a good man, and he voted out of duty, but he knew that he could not fully understand the issues that had been set out before him.

Beyond all these practical difficulties, there was an even sadder, and less frequently acknowledged, aspect to Fred's plight. Fred had been culturally deprived of the stimulation, the beauty, and the excitement that all civilized people—that is, all reading people—in all ages, and in all places, have taken as their birthright. He could not ever share in the wonders that had been created for him, in his own powerful and expressive language, by skillful and imaginative writers throughout the centuries. He was deaf to poetry, lost to the short story, and bereft of the consolations of the novel. He was doomed to a life of all "bread" and no "roses." And of course, Fred was not the worst case. He was not totally illiterate.

For the totally illiterate, the world is a twenty-four-hour minefield. Street signs and emergency roadside warnings are essentially mute. The directions on a bottle of medicine are an invitation to a life-and-death scenario. A letter from an old friend or relative is an inscrutable puzzle: Does it signify an inheritance? A death in the family? An old love rekindled? A debt being called in? The totally illiterate necessarily miss out on so much of what makes life worth living, and they are frequently doomed to bouts of unemployment, depression, and painful bewilderment in their personal lives.

Clearly, a free and democratic culture full of Freds and his totally illiterate compatriots cannot ultimately survive. Our education system has unfortunately produced in the last forty years a huge population of citizens who are marginally literate, unable to self-govern intelligently, and easy prey to either demagogues or chaos. This disheartening trend simply must be stopped; the richness of all of our future lives depends on our ability to stop it. America has always been the land of free speech, and Americans are vociferous about hating censorship of any kind, but there are worse, and more insidious dangers to our culture than overt book burnings. There is book neglect.

READING AS AN UNNATURAL BUT ESSENTIAL ACT

Turning the situation around won't be easy, but it should be fun and very satisfying. We just have to remember that reading is an "unnatural" act. Natural acts are instinctual, unconscious, and not particularly interesting, since they are shared by nearly everyone on the planet. Eating is a natural act; whether people eat with a fork, a knife and spoon, or chopsticks, however, is governed by the particular civilizations in which they grow up. It is an "unnatural," or "civilized," response to the simple need to eat.

Almost everything that human beings do that is truly interesting is unnatural in that sense. All of our juiciest gossip, stories, and jokes are centered around what is irregular, not quite natural. Anorexia and bulimia are considered interesting because they require considerable explanation, which the natural instinct to eat does not. The saintly desire to starve oneself and fast for enlightenment is also unnatural but quite intriguing. All humans eat, defecate, copulate, and dance. What is interesting is "how" they choose to do these things. Human nature has been fundamentally the same throughout time; what has changed is the thin veneer of civilization that has been skillfully applied over that raw and unfinished human nature.

Reading is an unnatural act in this sense because it too is artificial, learned, and governed by the society in which people grow up. Ants don't read, pigs don't read; even the best trained gorillas and chimpanzees are functionally illiterate. We don't want to find ourselves in a situation where most Americans are illiterate as well; it would seriously diminish our humanity. Unnatural acts define us as individual people and as a civilization. Lust is natural, but love is an unnatural act of the will, very much governed by the culture in which it occurs. Who would want to live without love? Who would want to forgo music? Who could bear to give up art and architecture? Who would want to be illiterate? Who would want to live like a natural beast?

Natural also means average, normal, and usual. Almost all art, or any great act of civilization, is created by people who are to a certain extent a bit unnatural themselves. That unnaturalness might be manifested in genius, eccentricity, or madness. Literature, myths, folklore, even our conversations around the water cooler, are usually about people who are different from the rest of us in some remarkable way. Normal, healthy people living quiet, staid lives, according to the rules of the particular situations in which they find themselves, are rarely sculptors or authors, or even the subjects of great statues or literature. It is that 2 percent, those geniuses and madmen whose perceptions are shaped by forces either above or below the norm, who are capable of creating art. And it is that next incredibly important part of the population, that next 20 percent, who are unnatural enough, civilized enough, to appreciate what the geniuses and madmen have created.

SO, WHAT KEEPS AMERICANS FROM READING?

Most Americans are not completely illiterate, so why don't those who can read make use of their skills? As Mark Twain so eloquently said over a hundred years ago, "The man who does not read good books has no advantage over the man who cannot read them." Why are so many literate Americans letting the advantages of the world of arts and letters pass them by?

To begin with, ours is a culture that offers many tantalizing distractions. It is no mere coincidence that the rise of the media coincides almost exactly with the fall of literacy rates in the United States. And truly, the media are wonderful. At any moment, in the privacy of his own home a typical middle-class American can turn on the radio and listen to AM or FM music, political commentary, or twenty-four-hour weather and traffic reports; he can choose to watch any one of over five hundred televisions channels, watching simultaneously *Gone with the Wind, Debbie Does Dallas,* and *Wild Kingdom;* and he can take a break to surf the Internet, buy a Pez dispenser on eBay, check a stock portfolio, or look up the symptoms of the latest fashionable disease. No wonder Americans are distracted and find it difficult to settle down and read.

Not only is media omnipresent, funneled directly into our homes, malleable on our computers, but its episodic nature, endlessly interruptible and resumable, makes it nearly impossible to ignore. Instant gratification is the name of the game, and our commercial advertisers play that game with consummate skill, much to the detriment of the average person's ability to focus, attend, and prioritize. It's too bad we couldn't occasionally follow the excellent example of Groucho Marx, who said over twenty years ago, "I find television very educating. Every time somebody turns on the set, I go into the other room and read a book."

The ironic thing is that with all these wonderful alternatives screaming for our attention, book sales are still up. This anomaly can largely be accounted for by the fact that it is the media's major job to sell things, including books. As Brian Lamb reports in *Booknotes,* "40 percent of all books bought in the United States are bought in the fourth quarter—the holiday season—and half of the books bought are never read."

So what about "reading" magazines and newspapers? Well, as long ago as the 1950s, Helen Haines, librarian extraordinaire, put those media in their proper perspective: "Magazines and newspapers—both dominant factors in American mass culture—are no more than accessories or deterrents to reading." In other words, they were the television and Internet of their time.

The media, however, cannot bear the full burden for our abandonment of reading and its many gifts. There are plenty of other ways to squander time and money in America. How about shopping? Or one of the most desirable of the seven deadly sins, gluttony? Given a choice between a five-star restaurant and a Pulitzer Prize–winning novel, the average person is quite likely to pick the restaurant. If it is a choice between osso bucco and *Oliver Twist,* or paella and *Pride and Prejudice,* more often than not the tasty dish is going to win.

Also, a convincing case can be made that the advent of amateur photography in America has been a major distraction, raised to the level of inescapable nuisance by the digital camera, which allows anyone, without any real effort, to take fairly good pictures. Digital photography fosters obsessive-compulsive behavior (having to get a picture of every single one of life's little moments, and then putting them neatly in albums or digital slide shows); narcissism (the average American has more photographs and home movies of himself to look at and admire than Queen Victoria would ever have thought possible); and an unreasonable preference for images rather than print as a source of information (making people unduly reliant on their eyes, as opposed to their reason or imagination).

In addition to all these distractions, there are many worthy pursuits in twenty-first-century life that also tend to estrange us from reading: politics, the arts, travel, chess, playing and listening to music, sports, and of course, sex. What is a thoughtful person to do? Well, usually, people manage to find time for things that are important to them. Reading is important. And as Anna Quindlen observed quite rightly, "While we pay lip service to the virtues of reading, the truth is that there is still in our culture something that suspects those who read too much, whatever reading too much means, of being lazy, aimless dreamers, people who need to grow up and come outside to where real life is, who think themselves superior in their separateness."

CONVINCING OURSELVES THAT READING IS WORTH PURSUING

What is it about literature that commands the attention of so many intelligent people, at all times, in every part of the world? Its rewards are many and obvious to those who are avid readers, but the pastime can seem frivolous to others. It is useful to take some time to articulate what good things can come from a lifetime affair with literature. People who can't see the profit in it surely won't pursue it.

The argument for reading good literature is really not very difficult to make, although in recent times it has not been made often enough, or forcefully enough, in our schools and homes. While people read for many different reasons, they all read to better themselves in one way or another.

The remainder of this introduction will take a look at some of the reasons people choose to spend their valuable time reading. One person might like to read to simply garner information, the kinds of things that make great players of Trivial Pursuit, Scrabble, or *Who Wants to Be a Millionaire?* Another reader might be interested in what makes people tick: What is going on in the mind of a mass murderer, a solitary housewife, a black intellectual? Still another person, who finds television a bit too passive, might just read for fun, a mentally active way to unwind after a long day at work. Some folks read to explore big ideas. Some read as a way to visit distant lands while sitting comfortably on their couches. Some love the suspense of a good mystery, and others read for the sheer beauty of the ways in which certain authors use the language. People read poetry and fiction for all kinds of reasons—all of them good. Here are a number of valid reasons to pursue a reading life, from some noteworthy sources:

"For me, life without reading would be like being in prison, it would be as if my spirit were in a straitjacket; life would be a very dark and narrow place" (Isabel Allende).

"In a very real sense, people who have read good literature have lived more than people who cannot or will not read. . . . It is not true that we have only one life to live; if we can read, we can live as many more lives and as many kinds of lives as we wish" (S. I. Hayakawa).

"The failure to read good books both enfeebles the vision and strengthens our most fatal tendency—the belief that the here and now is all there is" (Allan Bloom).

"I've never known any trouble that an hour's reading didn't assuage" (Charles de Secondat).

"The love of books is a love which requires neither justification, apology, nor defense. It is a good thing in itself; a possession to be thankful for, to rejoice over, to be proud of, and to sing praises for. With this love in his heart no man is ever poor, ever without friends, or the means of making his life lovely, beautiful, and happy" (John Alfred Langford).

"One can only snort so many ants and have so much sex before one starts to long for the comfort and companionship of a good book" (Moby, rock star).

"Reading is to the mind what exercise is to the body" (Sir Richard Steele).

"When I am attacked by gloomy thoughts, nothing helps me so much as running to my books. They quickly absorb me and banish the clouds from my mind" (Michel de Montaigne).

"The horror would be to have read all that was written, to have come to the end of books; a horror that prisoners and soldiers know, parceling out their few available books page by page, a page a day so as to last out the year" (Geoffrey O'Brien).

3

ELEVEN GOOD REASONS TO MAKE READING A PART OF YOUR LIFE

It is clear from the previous quotes that there are as many good reasons to read as there are good readers. The focus of this book will be the eleven reasons to read good literature most often cited by students, serious readers, critics, and authors.

Each reason presented will be preceded by an icon, which will then be used in the annotated section of the book that follows, to help direct readers immediately to books most likely to best serve their current reading needs.

READING FOR INFORMATION

One thing that the modern world is full of is information. A quick surf of the channels on TV gives us a chance to learn about laser surgery, hummingbird behavior, volcanoes of the world, Egyptology, gardening, or high-powered weapons. And those are just some of the topics on the "education" channels. On the Internet, we can find out about low-rate mortgages, Viagra, and Britney Spears, just by opening our spam e-mail. There are magazines edited especially for shutterbugs, dog breeders, would-be fashionistas, and news junkies. We also learn a lot of things at work: What's a toner cartridge? Is a director of marketing higher or lower than the vice president of finance? How can one tell the difference between the common cold and a serious flu? When is the exact right time to read someone their Miranda rights? There is information—or more exactly, data—everywhere. But where is knowledge?

Knowledge, or information that has meaning, can be found in a number of places, but especially in books of fiction. We can savor a very long novel like Melville's *Moby Dick,* in which Captain Ahab scours the world's seas looking for his nemesis, the great white whale, and find an encyclopedic knowledge of the nineteenth-century whaling industry: how to identify different whales; different methods of capture and preservation; uses for whale bone, whale oil, and ambergris; sailing and navigational principles; important whaling ports of the world; and the economics of whaling. But more than that, the book recreates what it was like to be on the high seas in the early days of navigation, how men lived together in cramped quarters for months at a time, and why whaling was a significant industry in America in the 1900s. *Moby Dick* offers us more than just a bunch of scattered, unrelated facts; it offers a real understanding of whaling and all its aspects; it offers knowledge.

In a similar way, we can approach Shakespeare not just to revel in his gorgeous language but also to acquire practical knowledge about politics, bird behavior, running a theater, the fabric industry, military strategy, and coinage, to name just a few of the subjects about which Shakespeare was particularly knowledgeable.

As Thomas Carlyle said over 150 years ago, "The true University of these days is a collection of books." It is even more true today that almost anything a reader wants to learn about can be understood deeply and thoroughly through good books.

Example of a Good Book to Read Primarily for Information

Mark Bailey's *The Saint.* This novel imagines what would happen if a genetics laboratory in San Diego resurrected the memory of the biblical St. Peter in a modern man. Along the way there's plenty of inside information about the high-tech world of genetic research, and the equally complicated spiritual and political realm of the Vatican.

READING TO UNDERSTAND OTHERS

What if there were a group that we could join that would ensure that we would meet hundreds of fascinating people in the next few years? These would be people whom we would get to know intimately—doctors, cowboys, housewives, murderers, and saints. And even better, we would be promised that none of these people would harm us in any way, just enrich our lives with their perceptions and experiences. Avid readers constitute such a fortunate group, and we can join them in the quest to understand others.

Most of us, in our daily lives, have family and a few good friends, with some coworkers and acquaintances thrown in for good measure. The number of really amazing people whom we can know personally is limited by our time, energy, station in life, and tolerance for risk. The narrow perspective we inevitably acquire from our daily lives usually makes us a bad judge of character when we try to figure out the motivations of strangers or those outside our immediate sphere of human understanding. As Israel Zangwill so justly observes, "The average taxpayer is no more capable of grand passion than of a grand opera."

Take a simple concept like love. We know what it means, right? Well, certainly, we know what it means to us. But what does it mean to others? Literature can give us an infinite number of answers to such important questions as this. If we read André the Chaplain's *The Art of Courtly Love,* we will be aware that some people think of love as just an elaborate and civilized game. If we consider Dante's *Divine Comedy* we will know intimately a man whose love for an underage girl made him consider love to be a purely spiritual and not physical involvement. If we've read Chaucer's *Canterbury Tales,* we've met the Wife of Bath, who saw love only as an all-out war between the sexes, which she intended to win. And if we've read or seen Shakespeare's *Romeo and Juliet,* we know that some people consider love a very serious family concern, not a personal matter at all. Sinclair Lewis's Babbitt (in his book of that name) liked to think of love as a convenient arrangement for living a simple, uneventful, middle-class life; Katherine Anne Porter, for her part, would not stoop to calling anything love that was not a totally engrossing, passionate engagement of the whole person, body and soul. In order to appreciate fully how other people understand love without unduly disrupting our own domestic relations, we need only take out a good book.

Literature is enjoyable primarily because it is about human beings. Even when a book seems to be about animals or robots, we are interested in these critters or automatons because of the human qualities they display. Literature presents many typical human situations and a wide sampling of the ways different people have tried to deal with them. The more we have read, the more likely that we will be prepared to deal with new and unusual situations in our own lives. The more options that we are aware of, the more people we have read about and know intimately, the more likely that we will be capable of dealing with others, not just on our own limited terms but with a broader understanding of their perspectives as well.

Whatever the real conditions of our lives, we can feel the frustration and bitterness of blacks through Eldridge Cleaver, the fear of entombment with Edgar Allen Poe, the joys of Christian fellowship with Jonathan Edwards, and many other emotions perhaps not regular parts of our lives.

Whatever the state of our minds, we can explore the psychologies of others through reading. How does a classic schizophrenic think? Read *Three Faces of Eve,* or *Sybil,* or *Psycho* to find out. What kinds of men rob and kill an entirely defenseless rural family? Read Truman Capote's *In Cold Blood.* How does a man obsessively in love with a terrible woman deal with his situation? Read Somerset Maugham's *Of Human Bondage.* There's no human psychology that hasn't been thoroughly explored by some author, at some time. There is no turn of mind that cannot be empathized with, as is shown so brilliantly in Nabokov's *Lolita,* which even makes child abuse explicable (though obviously still inexcusable).

It is also important to remember that while history is written by the victors, literature often tells the equally important story of the victimized. In *One Flew Over the Cuckoo's Nest, Slaughterhouse Five,* and *Woman on the Edge of Time,* we hear from the wrongly institutionalized, the reluctant soldier, and the oppressed minority—the very people who are unfortunately overlooked in the wide panorama of historical events.

Example of a Good Book to Read Primarily for an Understanding of Others

Harper Lee's *To Kill a Mockingbird.* This book makes a strong case for the idea that we never know another person until we have walked a mile in their shoes.

READING TO KNOW ONESELF

Socrates said, "Know thyself." It is a simple formulation, difficult of execution. People walk around happily displaying bracelets engraved WWJD, confident that they know "What Would Jesus Do," but at the same time they find themselves at a loss to answer a simpler question, much closer to home—WWID, "What Would I Do?" A strong sense of "What Would I Do" in any given situation is what is largely missing in many Americans' lives. People scramble from crisis to crisis, without any self-awareness or rock-solid principles to guide them. Where do such helpful principles and self-awareness come from? On the religious side, there are many churches waiting to guide us. On the secular side, literature can be a huge help. In the words of Clifton Fadiman, "When you re-read a classic you do not see more in the books than you did before; you see more in you than there was before."

Reading good books encourages us to identify and enrich our authentic interests. We define what we are, and are not, by looking into the telling mirror of literature. Books give readers a chance to ask, over and over again, in a million hypothetical situations, what would I do? For example, in the great American epic *Gone with the Wind,* Scarlett O'Hara is confronted by the loss of her ancestral home, the advent of the Civil War, the loss of her only child, a series of failed marriages, and the love of a wicked and wonderful man, Rhett Butler. We cannot help but assess the choices that Scarlett makes during the course of the novel and ask ourselves seriously what we might have done in her place to save our family home, keep our independence, survive a war, and meet our emotional and financial needs.

Reading is also a way of putting our own lives and selves in proper perspective. Reading about people whose lives are more deprived, more damaged, more chaotic, or more arduous than ours can make us appreciate the things that we can be thankful for. Reading about people whose lives are more interesting, more meaningful, more successful, or more fun than ours can inspire us to want to achieve more, and they can help us find the quickest routes to that achievement. Reading is a sure way of fitting ourselves into the hierarchy of things and seeing where we stand, and if that is where we want to stand.

Reading is additionally one of the few socially acceptable solitary endeavors. It's a pleasurable way to retreat from the activities and people of our lives—both physically and psychologically. Knowing oneself not only takes time, it takes privacy, and also a habit of introspection that can be developed through a healthy love of solitude, in which we can take the time to read and think. Readers are those lucky folks who can be alone without being lonely. They do not always require other people to entertain them. Many a beleaguered captive has survived his captivity through the power of books, the memory of good books, and the ability to think and spend time profitably alone. We can be intellectually independent like them and survive the dreaded doctor's waiting room with enviable poise and serenity, as long as we have a good book with us.

And finally, literature is a sure path to that very mysterious, but much talked about, quality of "self-esteem." Readers feel good about their ability to enter into any conversation, keep their minds alive in trying circumstances, and to "get the joke." Self-esteem does not come from kindly teachers telling Fred that he is a nice boy; it comes from Fred tackling challenging projects, recognizing his failures, and experiencing some measure of personal success. Being a well-read, literate person in our declining culture is a genuine cause for considerable self-esteem, and everyone knows it. It answers what Harold Bloom calls the human "search for a difficult pleasure."

Example of a Good Book to Read Primarily
for an Understanding of Oneself

Edward Albee's *Who's Afraid of Virginia Woolf?* In this play, two couples play out the stresses of their respective marriages in a volatile night of drinking and conversation. We will be hard pressed not to ask ourselves what we might have said or done in George's or Martha's position.

READING FOR FUN

Ironically, many students learn to dislike reading right in school. High school teachers, afraid of being considered frivolous, or tied to outdated course outlines mandated by their schools, frequently spend all their time teaching tragedies, forgetting that there is a whole literature of laughter to explore. College professors of literature often fill their courses with turgid classics, which appeal to their scholarly proclivities but aren't really all that interesting to fledgling readers. Students bogged down with "assigned" reading never get a chance to gravitate to the books that appeal to their adolescent sensibilities or to explore their own particular youthful interests. No wonder nobody is having any fun. It's time to remember that a great deal of superb literature is excruciatingly funny and that a satisfying part of being an educated person is being able to "get the joke."

From Aristophanes to Woody Allen, there are plenty of worthy authors who tackle serious questions in amusing ways. Humor itself is a topic of incredible interest, as it is well known that one person's hysterical joke is another person's boring nightmare. The person who loves Calvin Trillin's gentle humor might find P. J. O'Rourke rather harsh, Tom Robbins a little obscene, and Roy Blount just silly. Finding the exact authors who tickle our funny bone is part of the enjoyment of reading.

A book can also be a light-hearted friend. As Holbrook Jackson points out in *The Anatomy of Bibliomania*, "Books are never out of humour; never envious or jealous, they answer all questions with readiness . . . they dispel melancholy by their mirth, and amuse by their wit." Modern medical literature is focusing more and more on the salutary effects of laughter on good health and healing. We should go ahead and give ourselves permission to read a funny book; it's good for us.

Example of a Good Book to Read Primarily for Fun

Martin Amis's *Money: A Suicide Note. Money* is a scathingly funny send up of the 1980s, an exposé of the nouveau riche, of their excesses and their complete cluelessness.

READING FOR IDEAS

Some people are genuinely interested in the big ideas. These folks have a theoretical bent that might be satisfied by reading the great philosophers, the important social thinkers, or the important works of world religions. Other people like to explore the big ideas through the microcosm of individual lives. Literature is the natural path to metaphysics for them.

We all have a personal philosophy, whether we have worked on it consciously or not. For many it is a kludged-together hodge-podge of ideas gathered from our parents, our school experiences, the prejudices of our times, and television commercials. For a few of us, our life philosophy is a conscious work-in-progress, crafted out of the insights of philosophers, the principles of major religious traditions, heady conversations with our peers, and the ideas we get from the great body of the world's literature.

Most philosophers have turned, at one time or another, to storytelling to make their insights accessible to more people. Jesus, Buddha, and Mohammed all told stories to their disciples to help clarify and spread their ideas. In modern times, the existentialists rarely wrote nonfiction tracts of straight philosophy but preferred to let their ideas unfold in works like Camus's novel *The Stranger*, or Sartre's play *No Exit*.

Whatever the state of our own personal philosophies, we can always explore the ideas of others as expressed in their works. Thomas Hardy's novels, like *Jude the Obscure*, for example, are full of the philosophy of predestination, in which he firmly believed. Ayn Rand brought her objectivist philosophy to America through the characters in her novels like *The Fountainhead* and *Anthem.* Flannery O'Connor expressed her own brand of southern Christianity in short stories like "A Good Man Is Hard to Find" and "Everything That Rises Must Converge." Even authors whose main intent is not to promote a particular philosophical point of view often stop to ponder important ideas in the course of their narratives. We can garner useful ideas from literature that we might never have cooked up in the laboratories of our own minds.

In 1906 Edward Bulwer-Lytton made the following suggestion to the readers of the *Times Literary Supplement:* "Do you want to get at new ideas? Read old books. Do you want to find old ideas? Read new ones." Old books, new books—the important thing is that so many books are full of so many remarkable ideas. And we shouldn't overlook science fiction, which is one of the most idea-filled genres of modern literature. Orwell's *1984,* Card's *Ender's Game,* Dick's *Do Androids Dream of Electric Sheep?* and Huxley's *Brave New World* are classics of speculative thought.

Probably the best expression of what to do with the ideas found in books is this observation of Maxine Hong Kingston's: "I don't just record ideas when I read, I contend with the ideas the book presents; I work with them, engage in combat with them, synthesize them into concepts I already know, and then come up with my own ideas."

Example of a Good Book to Read Primarily for Ideas

Gita Mehta's *A River Sutra.* The main character of this thoughtful novel seeks personal enlightenment with the help of his clerk, his friend the mullah, and passing pilgrims who share his quest, and sometimes his otherwise quiet life.

READING AS VIRTUAL TRAVEL

We are all products of the time and place in which we are born. Through reading, we can escape the boundaries of geography and the limits of our age, and travel virtually anywhere, anytime.

Are we on a limited budget but still have an incredible wanderlust? Do we like to know something ahead of time about the places we are actually traveling to? Do we like to visit first, and then reflect on our experiences later, by comparing them with the travels of others? Do we like to do all our traveling from a comfy armchair? However we use literature to enhance our travel experience, it can open a window for us onto the entire world.

Nobody can show us Spain or take us to the bullfights like Ernest Hemingway. Nobody can share an African sunrise with us like Isak Dinesan. Nobody is better company in the drawing rooms of England than Henry James. And nobody can give us a better idea of what it's like to wander the streets of New York, with no money in our pockets, than James Leo Herlihy. As Kareem Abdul-Jabbar says, "Whenever I travel somewhere, the fact that I've read a lot about wherever I go enables me to understand what I am seeing and where I am. I get a lot more out of traveling." We enrich our travels by taking Mary Renault's *The Mask of Apollo* to Athens, Michener's *Alaska* to the fiftieth state, and the Bible to the Holy Land. We can read our way to a deeper and more sophisticated understanding of our world, even as we travel in it.

It is also true that whenever we happen to have been born, we can also still relive the past, or pre-guess the future, through literature. We can take the time to discover nineteenth-century Paris with Victor Hugo in *The Hunchback of Notre Dame* or contemplate a *Brave New World* with Aldous Huxley. Relive the age of chivalry with Sir Thomas Malory, or go directly to 2061 with Arthur Clarke. Either direction we travel in time, literature lets us escape the confines of our own particular moment and explore the realities of other eras. Thomas Carlyle got it just right when he wrote, "In books lies the soul of the whole Past Time; the articulate audible voice of the past, when the body and material substance of it has altogether vanished like a dream." We can only add, and the Future Time too.

Example of a Good Book to Read Primarily for Virtual Travel

Vonnegut's *Slaughterhouse Five*. Billy Pilgrim is unstuck in time, and traveling with him we can go back and visit the Dresden fire-bombings of World War II and see him as an infantryman, as well as participate in his vivid alien abduction into the future.

READING TO BECOME A PART OF OUR CULTURE

What is the point of living in America today, where we have relatively free access to books, if we don't take advantage of that access and actually read? When we look at the sacrifices people have made in other parts of the world to read and write surreptitiously, in fear of persecution, it is remarkable that Americans do not take more advantage of their precious freedoms.

Censors, who would like to limit our access to books, are always on the horizon. History is an intermittent story of outbreaks of censorship, from the burning of the great library of Alexandria in Egypt through the Catholic Church's Index of Forbidden Books, to the political-correctness movement in twenty-first-century America. How can we distinguish ourselves from disadvantaged people living in repressive regimes who are denied all of the satisfactions we have been discussing? There's only one way—we must take advantage of our cultural rights, and read. As Ray Bradbury, the prescient writer of *Fahrenheit 451,* the great science fiction book about censorship, said in 1994, "You don't have to burn books to destroy a culture. Just get people to stop reading them." Bradbury is, of course, correct; it is the very viability of our culture that is at stake. Dead languages are dead only because no one any longer speaks them. Dead cultures are dead only because no one any longer reads their books, plays their music, enjoys their arts, or lives by their values.

The more we read, the more we become part of our culture and also an important part of the process of transmitting that culture to the next generation. We partake more fully in the life of our times, and we share an important common intellectual and cultural background with other thoughtful people living around us. Authors have their fingers on the national and international jugular. Readers are usually ahead of the curve when it comes to predicting cultural shifts and political realities. They are, quite simply, "in the loop." As Barbara Tuchman writes, "Books are the carriers of civilization. Without books, history is silent, literature dumb, science crippled, thought and speculation at a standstill."

Full cultural participation requires some familiarity with the classics of our language. While the evening newspaper might provide conversation for the next day's lunch hour, a close reading of Shakespeare's *Hamlet* provides a lifetime of food for thought, and an immediate bond with other literate people of our age. As Ezra Pound observed in the *ABC of Reading,* "Literature is news that stays news." There are certain basic texts of Western literature that every reader would do well to know. The list may vary from critic to critic, but it often contains classics like Sophocles' *Antigone,* the book of Job in the Bible, Dante's *Divine Comedy,* Chaucer's *Canterbury Tales,* Milton's *Paradise Lost,* Shakespeare's *Macbeth,* Henry James's *Portrait of a Lady,* Flaubert's *Madame Bovary,* Dostoyevski's *Crime and Punishment,* Thoreau's *Walden Pond,* and Dickens's *Great Expectations.* If we haven't had a chance to read any of these books yet, we shouldn't be discouraged. Just remember what Samuel Butler said, "The oldest books are still only just out to those who have not read them." We have the joys of reading the classics ahead of us.

Also, full cultural participation includes reading modern works by cutting-edge authors and helping to decide, with our reading dollars, which books will be the classics of the future. It's no surprise that the books that survive from century to century are the books that have the wide readerships that make continuous publication commercially profitable.

We should also watch out for those very special books that actually foster cultural and social change in the real world. For example, Upton Sinclair's *The Jungle,* which described with brutal realism the conditions in the stock houses of Chicago in the 1900s, brought about the Federal Food and Drug Administration, which protects not only modern butchers and cows but modern consumers as well. Charles Dickens had a special mission to call attention to the abuses of his age; his novels like *Bleak House* and *Hard Times* created real changes in the English legal system and helped to improve conditions in orphanages, schools, and debtors' prisons, all of which were reformed in his lifetime. President William J. Clinton, a Rhodes Scholar, was very sensitive to the role books play in any culture: "Where books are preserved, studied and revered, human beings will also be treated with respect and dignity, and liberty will be strengthened."

And finally, there is an important interplay between literature and the other arts. Literature makes music, theater, painting, sculpture, architecture, and even the media more enjoyable and meaningful. For example, there is no question that movies are one of the major art forms of our time. Reading the books from which many movies are made enriches our experience of them, provides deeper understanding of character motivation, and exercises our powers of comparison. We should never think that we do not need to read a book because we have seen the movie; equally, we should never think we do not need to see a movie because we have read the book. Raymond Chandler, the famous American mystery novelist, understood the relationship between movies and novels better than anyone: "If my books had been any worse, I should not have been invited to Hollywood, and . . . if they had been any better, I should not have come."

Example of a Good Book to Read Primarily to Become a Part of Your Culture

Editor Louise Erdrich's *The Best American Short Stories 1993.* Every year, hundreds of the best new short stories are published in literary magazines like *Harper's, Antaeus, The Paris Review,* and *The New Yorker.* At the end of the year, several anthologies of short fiction are edited from these sources; *The Best American Short Stories* is one of the most admired of these compilations.

READING FOR SUSPENSE

Literature also shares some of the appeal of a football game or any other exciting sport. Spectators and readers both want to know "what happens next!" In the classic *Thousand and One Nights* (or *The Arabian Nights*), King Shahryar has a habit of bringing beautiful women to his bed and killing them before the morning. One night Shahrazad is brought to him, and she begins to tell him an interesting tale of romance and intrigue. Each night just before completing her story, she stops her tale at the most suspenseful moment and lets the king know that she will tell him the ending the following night. Each night, she honors her promise to complete the preceding night's story, but she also begins a new one, equally suspenseful, and breaks off once more right before the conclusion. This goes on for the infamous 1,001 nights. It is a shame that Shahrazad eventually runs out of stories, but her unusual survival technique is a testament to the compelling power of suspense in literature.

There are some readers for whom this motive is so strong that the only books they read are detective or mystery novels. Curiosity leads them from page to page, and they are equally pleased when they guess the outcome correctly and validate their own intelligence, as when the author gives them an interesting surprise and shows them possibilities they had never thought of before. Suspense is the quality that makes it difficult to put a book down, and most good authors trade on its strengths to some degree.

Example of a Good Book to Read Primarily for Suspense

Agatha Christie's *The Murder of Roger Ackroyd*. In this mystery novel Hercule Poirot, who has gone into retirement in the sleepy English village of King's Abbot, is drawn into one of the most complex mysteries of his career.

READING FOR THE LOVE OF BEAUTY

Words, of course, are everyone's common property, but the order of words often has magic in them. We all enjoy seeing thoughts we've perhaps had ourselves perfectly expressed. In Henry James's *The American,* the main character, Christopher Newman, has been wandering around the Louvre museum in Paris for hours and finally collapses onto a cushion in the Grande Salon with an "aesthetic headache." Anyone who has ever pushed himself or herself beyond endurance in an enormous, world-class museum will feel immediately the perfection of that phrase.

The Bible says, "In the beginning was the Word," and there are many anthropologists who feel that written language, and not the opposable thumb, is what distinguishes us from the animals. At least, it is undeniably true that literature fills a need in us for beauty, a need that is distinctively human.

There are many ways in which we bring beauty into our lives, and ideally each of us has at least one means that is particularly precious. There is the austere beauty of line and form in drawing. There is the vibrancy and nuance of color in painting. There is the differing tonality of Western and Eastern music. There is the contemplation of an elegant mathematical equation. There is the wonder of mass and space in architecture. There is the absolute beauty of a well-executed basketball shot. And, of course, there is the aesthetic beauty of a well-turned phrase, the arabesque intricacies of plot, and the "Aha" we feel when we think, "I wish I'd said that, just that way!"

One of the reasons that we can often return to our favorite books even when we know how the plot turns out is the pleasure we take in the pure beauty of the book's language or form. No one buys a painting by Van Gogh, puts it on the wall for a few days, and then throws it away. Things of real beauty can be returned to over and over again; their perfection continues to astonish. The great painter Van Gogh himself put it this way: "It is with the reading of books the same as with looking at pictures; one must, without a doubt, without hesitations, with assurance, admire what is beautiful." That is also a good reminder to us that there is a great deal of beauty in the artwork and photographs that we find in children's books, books of poetry, and other illustrated literature.

Example of a Good Book to Read Primarily for the Love of Beauty

Tom Robbins's *Even Cowgirls Get the Blues.* It is difficult to think of any other modern author who has loved the beauty of the English language as ardently and faithfully as Tom Robbins.

READING FOR GLIMPSES OF PERFECTION

Most religions caution us that perfection does not exist on earth, but they also hold out perfection as a worthy goal to strive toward. They frequently describe an other-worldly afterlife, or heaven, where perfection will finally be realized by virtuous followers. There is certainly a yearning in the human heart for glimpses of a perfect life, world, and universe. We long to live for awhile in the ideal, where women are always beautiful, men always true, and dogs never get run over in the streets.

The large body of utopian works in literature is a product of this impulse to glimpse the flawless. The ancient Greek philosopher Plato tried to imagine a perfect state in his *Republic,* and Thomas More popularized the word *utopia* (Latin for nowhere) in his sixteenth-century classic of the same name. Throughout time, authors have been trying to construct, or imagine, hermetically sealed societies in which perfection might possibly flourish.

However, just as we all have different senses of humor, we also have different ideas about what a perfect society, or life, might look like. In *Walden Pond,* Thoreau rhapsodizes about the satisfactions of solitude and a return to the rhythms of nature; one hundred years later, B. F. Skinner, in *Walden Two,* applies behaviorist theories to create a society in which many people can live in harmony through systematic psychological conditioning. James Hilton, in *Lost Horizon,* tells of an airplane crash, high on a mysterious Tibetan plateau, where the Western crew is saved by the monks of Shangri-La and shown an Eastern paradise, which some of them love and some hate. In Charlotte Perkins Gilman's *Herland,* three male explorers similarly get lost, but they happen instead on an all-female, feminist utopia and are forced to rethink their assumptions about women's roles and abilities. Edward Bellamy, writing in the nineteenth century in *Looking Backward: 2000–1887,* puts his utopia in the year 2000, by having a Victorian Bostonian wake up a hundred years later in a world of remarkable prosperity and harmony. Huxley, better known for his dystopia *Brave New World,* once tried to imagine a perfect society in his novel *Island,* which is an interesting mélange of Buddhism, tantric sexuality, and drugs.

It is not surprising that Huxley might approach the problem of perfection from both sides, as Harold Bloom observed: "Dystopias teach us about perfection by exploring its exact opposite or shadow side." Many writers have tried to point the direction to perfection by exploring imperfection. Probably one of the most famous dystopias is George Orwell's *1984,* with its grim totalitarian state, where Big Brother is always watching and the Thought Police are ever vigilant to root out unorthodoxy. Equally disturbing is Samuel Butler's *Erewhon* (Nowhere "almost" spelled backward), in which the fear of machines is elevated to an overriding social paranoia. And as a counterpoint to *Herland,* Margaret Atwood's *The Handmaid's Tale* is a feminist dystopia in which every aspect of women's lives, including childbirth, is controlled by men.

While dystopias reveal our worst fears, utopian literature gives us a chance to contemplate how things ought to be, as opposed to the way they frequently are. As Aldous Huxley, the acknowledged expert in this genre, said, "Real orgies are never so exciting as pornographic books. In a volume by Pierre Louys all the girls are young and their figures perfect; there's no hiccoughing or bad breath, no fatigue or boredom, no sudden recollections of unpaid bills or business letters unanswered, to interrupt the raptures. Art gives you the sensation, the thought, the feeling quite pure—chemically pure, I mean . . . not morally." Or as George Bernard Shaw says it more simply, "Only in books has mankind known perfect truth, love and beauty."

Example of a Good Book to Read Primarily for Glimpses of Perfection

Marge Piercy's *Woman on the Edge of Time.* When Connie Ramos time travels into the future, she finds that a utopian, agrarian society is competing for survival with a brutal, technological totalitarian state.

READING TO DEVELOP THINKING, WRITING, AND CONVERSATIONAL SKILLS

Thinking

Literature cultivates our vanishing ability to pay attention, focus with our full being, and think coherently. There are many enemies of attention in the modern world: nightly news, game shows, commercials, the Internet, the stock market, and everything that rushes at us in fifteen-second sound bites or quick glimpses. A love of reading is a foolproof cure for what Donald Tovey calls the "Age of Inattention."

Literature also forces us to use our faculties of imagination, which are rarely otherwise called upon. Like other faculties, imagination is enhanced through constant use, and a well-exercised imagination can be an asset in almost any setting. Even music, which used to be one of the great spurs to imagination in our culture, has been co-opted by the slick image makers of MTV and VH1. Once we have seen a music video of a popular song, it is difficult to have our own creative ideas about it any more. Our imaginations are repeatedly undermined by an overheated media, and we surrender our active thinking for passive watching. Unless we regain our ability to imagine for ourselves, we will never be out there with suspense novelist Tom Clancy in saying, "I've made up stuff that's turned out to be real, that's the spooky part."

Writing

The French writer Jean-Paul Sartre might be overstating the case a little bit, but there is certainly some truth in his notion that "in reality, people read because they want to write." A great many readers eventually try their hand at writing or are inspired to write by something they have read. The poet George Elliot Clarke swears that he "would never have attempted poetry were it not for that book [*Play Ebony Play Ivory*] with its red-bordered, white-print-against-a-black-background cover and its paradise of African-nuanced, Southern-bluesy, Harlem-jazzy, imagist, surrealist, swinging poems." Reading is a great generator of ideas, a tremendous motivation to express ourselves as well as we are able.

For those who write as well as read, literature affords an extra pleasure, because constant, careful reading cannot help but improve our writing ability. It enlarges our vocabularies, sharpens our minds, and activates our imagination and creative abilities. When we need to say something forcefully, our reading will aid us in our search for the right word, the correct argument, or the most effective image to get our ideas and feelings across to others. Charles Kuralt, until his death in 1997 a first-rate thinker on CBS News, explained it this way, "I can hear the rhythms of writers I admire when I sit down to write. . . . I do think that's how young writers learn . . . from growing very enthusiastic about something they're reading."

One last important, and sometimes overlooked, aspect of writing is fluency. Fluency is our ability to get words to flow easily and naturally. Everyone gets writer's block sometime, as Lu Chi points out in the *Art of Writing:* "Sometimes the words come freely; sometimes we sit in silence, gnawing on a brush," but a good reader is usually a good writer, who can easily generate beautiful and fitting words whenever necessary.

Conversation

Czech writer Kosta Bagakis in *Speaking of Reading* explained the relationship between reading, writing, and conversation in the strongest possible terms: "I maintain that reading is a social act. A book won't stay in my head unless I tell a friend about it, so I like to find other people to read the books I'm reading so we can talk about the ideas together. Sometimes, it's as if we've read different books, our ideas are so different. I have never read a book without sharing it with others—never." People who think that readers are solitary misfits who never venture beyond their bookshelves have it exactly wrong. Most readers enjoy good company, and make excellent company themselves.

Really charming conversationalists and raconteurs (storytellers) are even rarer today than avid readers, but we all appreciate them when we come across them. Many of our best nonfiction writers are beloved because of their ability to tell a story as well as any novelist could. In fact, the only difference Tom Clancy sees between fiction and reality is that "fiction has to make sense." What a joy it would be to sit down to a good dinner and have a conversation with Witold Rybczynski *(Home: A Short History of an Idea)*, Barbara Ehrenreich *(Nickel and Dimed: On [Not] Getting By in America)*, Tom Wolfe *(The Electric Kool-Aid Acid Test)*, Hunter Thompson *(Fear and Loathing in Las Vegas: A Savage Journey to the Heart of the American Dream)*, or Oliver Sacks *(The Man Who Mistook His Wife for a Hat: And Other Clinical Tales)*. What a joy it would be to sit down to a good meal with someone who has even read these stylish authors!

Southern writer and teacher Flannery O'Connor once recalled, "Everywhere I go I'm asked if I think the university stifles writers. My opinion is that they don't stifle enough of them." Or as she puts it in another way, "There's many a bestseller that could have been prevented by a good teacher." It's not difficult to tell that O'Connor would have been fun to talk to inside, or outside, of a classroom.

Example of a Good Book to Read Primarily for Thinking, Writing, and Conversational Skills

Oscar Wilde's *The Picture of Dorian Gray*. Oscar Wilde was a well-known wit and man-about-town, qualities we can appreciate in his suave main character, Lord Henry Wotton, in *Dorian Gray*.

II

A GOOD PLACE TO START

4

KEY TO THE
ANNOTATED BOOK LIST

This book list can be used in as many ways as there are individual readers. Some readers may want to skip this section and go directly to the book recommendations and browse at their leisure. Others may want to see exactly what each section of the annotations is about; they will probably stop and read the following explanations. This is a good place for readers to begin to follow their own inclinations and find patterns of book selection that work for them.

Title

Here readers will find the *exact title* of the work being recommended. It is easy to find a reading copy of the book being reviewed by plugging the exact title into the search engine of a favorite book source (for example, www.amazon.com, www.bn.com, www.ebay.com, www.booksalefinder.com), or by looking the title up in the title catalog of the local school, public, or university library.

Author

Here readers will find the *exact name or pseudonym* of the author of the work. Libraries and bookstores often file their fiction by the author's last name, under headings like Literature (the classics), Fiction (contemporary best-sellers), Short Stories (short-story collections), or Drama (plays). If the book has an editor rather than an author, his or her name will appear with the term "Editor."

Genre

Here readers will find a description of the *type of book* they will be reading: novel, play, or short story. They will also get an idea of the *kind of story* they might encounter: science fiction, gothic, western, romance, or mystery. The notation "various" means that the book contains works in various genres or subject matters.

Number of Pages

Here readers will find the *total number of pages* in the work. Some readers have lots of time to read and want to tackle long and engrossing works; other readers have serious time constraints that make shorter books more attractive. The number of pages noted refers to the number of pages in the reviewed copy; it may differ slightly from the number of pages in the readers' book, which may be from a different edition or another publisher.

Date

Here readers will find the *copyright date* of the work. This date tells when a book was originally issued by the publisher, and it is useful in putting a work into the context of its times. The copyright date might be different from a *printing date,* which only tells when that physical copy was actually printed. The printing date may hint at whether a book is currently available or not. Good books, even classics, unfortunately go out of print regularly.

Level of Challenge

Sometimes readers are in the mood to read something intellectually challenging, but sometimes they just want a good book, light in content and weight, to take to the beach. The *level-of-challenge* ratings in this book are designed to help readers find a book that suits their current moods and abilities. All the works recommended here are first-rate books of their type—engaging to read and well worth the time it would take to read them.

5   Books with this rating are challenging masterworks of literature. The vocabulary may be demanding, the ideas profound, or the subject matter unfamiliar or controversial. Whatever the difficulties posed by these books and however much the reader understands at

first reading, these books always reward the readers' efforts tenfold. Books like these are enduring, to be read over and over with pleasure, and provide infinite topics of conversation among well-read people. They often have archetypical plots that recur in all literatures in all times.

Examples include: *Oedipus Rex* by Sophocles, *Hamlet* by Shakespeare, *Madame Bovary* by Flaubert, *Lolita* by Nabokov, *The Sound and the Fury* by Faulkner, and *Angels and Insects* by A. S. Byatt.

4   Books with this rating are works of literature with enduring qualities. These books are more accessible to the general reader, with intricate plots, arresting characters, vivid language, and provocative ideas. These books do not make as many demands on the readers' vocabulary or prior knowledge, but they often merit several readings and grow more precious with familiarity.

Examples include: *The Merchant of Venice* by Shakespeare, *Lady Chatterley's Lover* by D. H. Lawrence, *The Volcano Lover* by Susan Sontag, *Even Cowgirls Get the Blues* by Tom Robbins, and *The Robber Bride* by Margaret Atwood.

3   Books with this rating are thought provoking, full of interesting information, and, because the language is not above a high school reading level, can be profitably read by almost anyone. Often these books are written by journalists, historians, philosophers, or others whose main interest is in social reform, science, or politics, for instance, rather than literature. One learns a lot about others' concerns and ideas from books like these.

Examples include: *Sister Carrie* by Dreiser, *The Ladies Paradise* by Zola, *Animal Farm* by George Orwell, *Woman on the Edge of Time* by Marge Piercy, *Elmer Gantry* by Sinclair Lewis, and *Bleak House* by Dickens.

2   Books with this rating are fun and relaxing to read. They have reliable, formulaic, and satisfying plots. Westerns, romance novels, detective fiction, and science fiction often fall into this category. Undemanding vocabulary, familiar characters, and puzzling plots often make these books very entertaining.

Examples include: *Ender's Game* by Orson Scott Card, *Shane* by Jack Warner Schaefer, *Jurassic Park* by Michael Crichton, *Dance upon the Air* by Nora Roberts, and *The Complete Sherlock Holmes* by Sir Arthur Conan Doyle.

1   Books with this rating were originally written for children but have tremendous appeal for adults as well. The vocabulary is easy,

whimsical, or nonsensical. They stimulate a sense of wonder and adventure and often have a clear and useful moral.

Examples include: *Charlotte's Web* by E. B. White, *Winnie the Pooh* by A. A. Milne, *Alice in Wonderland* by Lewis Carroll, and *The Secret Garden* by Frances Hodgson Burnett.

Synopsis

Here readers will find out something about the characters, setting, ideas, and plot of the book. Some readers may be drawn to books about people who are like themselves or people they know; others might be interested in people who are decidedly different. Some readers will want to read about places to which they have already traveled, or they might want to learn about places they plan to visit in the future. They might want to see what other people think about a topic in which they are currently interested, or they might want to be exposed to a topic they have never thought about before. A book that appeals to the reader today may be different from one that seems enticing tomorrow. Readers can use this section to help match their current interests to the books being annotated.

Quotations

Here readers will be able to sample the author's writing style, through the actual voice of the narrator, speeches of key characters, or passages of remarkable poetry or wit. A number of the quotes will refer to reading, writing, or literature, reinforcing ideas presented in this book. Readers can profitably browse this section for ideas for their own writing, and can use the entire text like a book of relatively unknown quotations. Readers can listen directly to the author's voice and see if they want to hear more.

Reading Hints

Every book has its own particular difficulties and beauties. This section calls attention to themes, examines patterns of metaphor, notes peculiarities and excellences of style, hints at ideas or philosophies implicit in the works, and makes note of questions the reader might encounter. While this section is tailored to the work being reviewed, what the reader learns here can be applied to many of the other books being reviewed. In fact, a reader might use the entire text as a "how to read literature" guide, by just reading the hints contained in all of these sections.

Others by Author

Readers who find a special sympathy for an author often read a number of books by that author in quick succession. In this section of the annotation, readers will find other titles by the same author (with a description of the genre in parentheses, like this). The work being annotated may be a novel, but the works in the "Others by Author" section may be collections of short stories or poetry, memoirs, children's books, book of essays, or even a plays.

Movie(s)

Kurt Vonnegut once said that there were only two novels that had been successfully made into films. One was his own *Slaughterhouse Five,* and the other was Margaret Mitchell's *Gone with the Wind.* Movies made from literature can be judged by their faithfulness to the plot outline of the original work of literature, by their fidelity to the ideas or tone of the original text, or as works of art in their own right. However readers judge the movies that they see, this section will direct them to films that claim to be tied in some way to the works of literature under review.

Icons

Readers will find three of the following icons at the end of each annotation. Most of the works recommended here exhibit many more than just three of the qualities of literature discussed in the opening chapter; however, sometimes it is good to know which of the reasons for reading are dominant in the selection.

 Reading for Information

 Reading to Understand Others

 Reading to Know Oneself

 Reading for Fun

 Reading for Ideas

Reading as Virtual Travel

 Reading to Become a Part of Our Culture

 Reading for Suspense

 Reading for the Love of Beauty

 Reading for Glimpses of Perfection

 Reading to Develop Thinking, Writing, and Conversational Skills

5

ANNOTATED BOOK LIST

Title: *1984*
Author: George Orwell
Genre: Novel **Number of Pages:** 245 **Date:** 1949
Level of Challenge: 3
Synopsis:
1984 is a frighteningly prophetic novel, written in 1949 by a writer concerned about the physical and psychological weaknesses of fragile human beings in the face of the terrible effects of totalitarianism and other assaults on human dignity. The imaginative future that Orwell describes, with its Newspeak, Big Brother, economic disparity, and perpetual war is closer to reality today than it was in 1984. Scary stuff.
Quotations:
"In a lucid moment Winston found that he was shouting with the others and kicking his heel violently against the rung of his chair. The horrible thing about the Two Minutes Hate was not that one was obliged to act a part, but that it was impossible to avoid joining in. Within thirty seconds any pretense was always unnecessary." Page 16.
"Don't you see that the whole aim of Newspeak is to narrow the range of thought? In the end we shall make thought-crime literally impossible, because there will be no words in which to express it." Page 46.
"But you could not have pure love or pure lust nowadays. No emotion was pure, because everything was mixed up with fear and hatred. Their embrace had been a battle, the climax a victory. It was a blow struck against the party. It was a political act." Page 105.
Reading Hints:
Imagining the future, or alternative societies, is hard work. Writers who believe in the possibility of a better world than the present one create Utopias.

Writers who foresee a more horrible existence for humankind create dystopias. Readers might like to compare their ideas about the future with Orwell's. Current trends may play out the way he imagined, or not.

Others by Orwell: *Animal Farm* (novel), *Keep the Aspidistra Flying* (novel), and *Shooting an Elephant, and Other Essays* (essays).

Movie: *1984* (1984). Michael Radford, director. Starring John Hurt, Richard Burton, and Suzanna Hamilton.

Reading Icons:

Title: *Alaska*
Author: James A. Michener
Genre: Novel **Number of Pages:** 1,073 **Date:** 1988
Level of Challenge: 3
Synopsis:
Michener is famous for his gigantic, best-selling, multigenerational historical novels. *Alaska* begins with the formation of the North American continent; follows with the migration of the mastodon and the woolly mammoth across the Bering Strait; then populates the new lands with Athapascans, Aleuts, and Eskimos. It tells the exciting, and sometimes brutal, story of Russian colonization; examines the Gold Rush and the early American settlers; and finally speculates on the post–World War II military and geographic importance of the forty-ninth state. A human face is put on all this history through the interlaced lives of prehistoric wanderers, Asiatic settlers, Russian fur traders, Boston whalers, Yukon miners, Alaskan bush pilots, World War II scouts, Japanese mountain climbers, and winners of the Iditarod.

Quotations:
"In this quiet way people can populate an entire continent by moving only a few thousand yards in each generation, if they are allowed twenty-nine thousand years in which to do it. They can move from Siberia to Arizona without ever leaving home." Page 57.

"In all, some sixty gold seekers perished that Sunday morning, but not even a disaster of such magnitude could diminish the passion with which the survivors hungered for gold or slow the incessant traffic up the mountain." Page 528.

"As always in a pioneer settlement, the heaviest burden fell upon the women, and when Elmer Flatch eschewed a chance for one of the attractive lots near the center of town—the ones that would be invaluable within a few years—selecting instead the romantic one near the glacier, his wife realized that the task of holding her family together while a cabin was being built and the children established in school would be hers." Page 800.

Reading Hints:

Readers will want to pay special attention to Michener's preface, "Fact and Fiction," in which he identifies which people in Alaska are real historical figures and which are fictional characters. In the preface, Michener also clarifies which geological, religious, biological, and archeological details were fact and which were still only theory when he wrote. (Bookmarking the map of Alaska and the Arctic Ocean is also a useful idea.)

Others by Michener: *The Source* (novel), *Chesapeake* (novel), and *Hawaii* (novel).

Reading Icons:

Title: *All the Pretty Horses*
Author: Cormac McCarthy
Genre: Novel **Number of Pages:** 302 **Date:** 1992
Level of Challenge: 2
Synopsis:

This is the story of John Grady Cole, a sixteen-year-old displaced rancher's son, with a profound love for horses and a wanderlust that takes him deep into Mexico looking for a true cowboy's life. McCarthy is an excellent writer, with the ability to describe landscape compellingly and to look deeply into the heart of a "strong, silent," young cowboy and see the courage, modesty. and goodness there.

Quotations:

"What he loved in horses was what he loved in men, the blood and the heat of the blood that ran them. All his reverence and all his fondness and all the leanings of his life were for the ardenthearted." Page 6.

"Bein' shot at will sure enough cause you to lose your appetite, won't it?" Page 85.

"A goodlookin' horse is like a goodlookin' woman, he said. They're always more trouble than what they're worth. What a man needs is just one that will get the job done." Page 89.

"Scars have the strange power to remind us that our past is real. The events that cause them can never be forgotten, can they?" Page 135.

Reading Hints:

In many novels the main character (protagonist) has a side-kick (foil), who is not so much interesting in himself but is a way of seeing and assessing the main character better. Rawlins in *All the Pretty Horses* is such a foil character. Only by comparison to him, a more typical youth on an adventure in Mexico, does the reader get to see how extraordinarily intelligent, talented, courageous, and ethical John Grady Cole really is.

Others by McCarthy: *The Crossing* (novel), *Blood Meridian* (novel), and *Child of God* (novel).

Movie: *All the Pretty Horses* (2000). Billy Bob Thornton, director. Starring Matt Damon, Penelope Cruz, and Henry Thomas.

Reading Icons:

Title: *American Gods*
Author: Neil Gaiman
Genre: Science Fiction Novel **Number of Pages:** 592 **Date:** 2001
Level of Challenge: 3
Synopsis:
There's a storm coming, and somehow Shadow has found himself in the middle of it all. On one side, the faltering old gods of the past and; on the other, the brash, new, cliché-ridden American icons. What a wild, strange trip it is through Gaiman's America, from roadside attractions to black limousines, from sacred to profane, from losing heart to having heart, and from middle America to the center of the universe. Hold on, it's a bumpy ride and then some.

Quotations:
"Tell him that we have fucking reprogrammed reality. Tell him that language is a virus and that religion is an operating system and that prayers are just so much fucking spam." Page 54.

"The important thing to understand about American history, wrote Mr. Ibis, in his leather-bound journal, is that it is fictional, a charcoal-sketched simplicity for the children, or the easily bored." Page 92.

"There are new gods growing in America, clinging to growing knots of belief; gods of credit card and freeway, of Internet and telephone, of radio and hospital and television, gods of plastic and of beeper and of neon." Pages 137–38.

"What I say is, a town isn't a town without a bookstore. It may call itself a town, but unless it's got a bookstore, it knows it's not fooling a soul." Page 252.

Reading Hints:
Gaiman's sprawling novel is all over the map, literally, in its use of international myth, folklore, and tall tales. Readers who are not familiar with this

kind of material might like to follow up on some of his allusions to "Thunderbirds," "Odin," "Ibis," "Marie Laveau," "Horus," and "Whiskey Jack," in reference books like Edith Hamilton's *Mythology,* Sir James George Frazer's *Golden Bough,* Joseph Campbell's *The Hero with a Thousand Faces,* or E. Hirsch's *The New Dictionary of Cultural Literacy.* All these books are packed with information and very interesting just to browse.

Others by Gaiman: *Neverwhere* (novel), *Preludes and Nocturnes* (adult comics), and *Stardust* (fairy tale).

Reading Icons:

Title: *As You Like It*
Author: William Shakespeare
Genre: Play Script **Number of Pages:** 31 **Date:** c. 1598
Level of Challenge: 5
Synopsis:
As You Like It is the quintessential Shakespearian comedy with plenty of mistaken identities, cross-dressing, brotherly rivalry, and love intrigues. Life at court is regal and corrupt, causing both Orlando and Rosalind to flee to the Forest of Arden, where pastoral values and inconveniences are in full swing. The many pairs of young lovers in the play have numerous escapades, which end, of course, in joyous wedding festivities.
Quotations:
"The more pity that fools may not speak wisely what wise men do foolishly." Page 364.
"Are not these woods/More free from peril than the envious court?" Page 368.
"If thou rememb'rest not the slightest folly/that ever love did make thee run into,/Thou hast not lov'd." Page 370.
"All the world's a stage,/and all the men and women merely players." Page 372.
Reading Hints:
The plots of Shakespeare's comedies are quite complicated. They rarely cause theatre-goers any problem, but they can sometimes confuse readers, because of all the twins, disguises, and characters with similar names. It is often helpful to read a simple synopsis of the plot before beginning a Shakespearian comedy. Marchette Chute's *Stories from Shakespeare* is a useful introductory book that supplies just enough information about each of Shakespeare's plays to get the reader started.

Others by Shakespeare: *Othello* (play), *Hamlet* (play), and *The Taming of the Shrew* (play).
Movies: *As You Like It* (1936). Paul Czinner, director. Starring Laurence Olivier, Elisabeth Bergner, and Felix Aylmer.
As You Like It (1978). BBC, director. Starring Helen Mirren, Angharad Rees, and Brian Stirner.

Reading Icons:

Title: *Balzac and the Little Chinese Seamstress*
Author: Dai Sijie
Genre: Novel **Number of Pages:** 197 **Date:** 2001
Level of Challenge: 3
Synopsis:
Two young boys, sons of bourgeois intellectuals, are caught up in Mao's Cultural Revolution in the early 1970s in China, and sent to Phoenix Mountain for political reeducation. In a small village they discover physical hardships, the lure of Western literature, their own sexuality, and an independence of mind and spirit never anticipated by the communist regime that sent them there.
Quotations:
"During the whole month of September following our successful burglary, we were seduced, overwhelmed, spellbound by the mystery of the outside world, especially the world of women, love and sex as revealed to us by these Western writers day after day, page after page, book after book." Page 115.
"It was insane, but the bourgeois intellectuals upon whom the Communists had inflicted so much hardship were no less strict morally than their persecutors." Page 176.
"At least having to trudge across the mountain . . . meant getting four days off from labouring in the fields, from carrying human and animal dung on our backs, or from toiling in the paddy fields with water buffalo whose long tails whacked you across the face." Page 85.
Reading Hints:
On the surface, *Balzac* is a simple and touching coming of age story, but readers who are observant about the details can also get a very good feel for the quality of life for ordinary Chinese citizens during Chairman Mao's ascendancy in China.
·rs by Sijie: None yet in English.

Reading Icons:

Title: *Bastard out of Carolina*
Author: Dorothy Allison
Genre: Novel **Number of Pages:** 309 **Date:** 1992
Level of Challenge: 3
Synopsis:
In gritty, unsentimental language, the young girl at the center of this story tells what it is like to grow up among out-of-control adults in the deep South of tent revivals, country/gospel music, desperate poverty, and uneducated people. It is a disturbing novel, containing scenes of violence and child abuse, but also a hopeful one, always returning to Aunt Raylene's philosophy that "Everybody just does the best they can." Page 258.
Quotations:
"A sad wounded man who genuinely likes women—that's what Earle is, a hurt little boy with just enough meanness in him to keep a woman interested." Pages 24–25.
"But it seemed like Daddy Glen's hands were always reaching for me, trembling on the surface of my skin, as if something pulled him to me and pushed him away at the same time." Page 105.
"That was what gospel was meant to do—make you hate and love yourself at the same time, make you ashamed and glorified. It worked on me. It absolutely worked on me." Page 136.
"Raylene had worked for the carnival like a man, cutting off her hair and dressing in overalls. She'd called herself Ray." Page 178.
Reading Hints:
One of the great innovations of twentieth-century literature was a movement away from telling the stories of kings and queens and other quite extraordinary people to the telling of stories of average people, even people whose behavior falls quite far below the norm. It turns out that the thoughts of the uneducated and the unwashed, killers and thieves, the infirm and the insane are every bit as interesting as the thoughts of their so-called betters.
Others by Allison: *Cavedweller* (novel), *Trash: Stories* (short stories), and *Two or Three Things I Know for Sure* (memoir).
Movie: *Bastard out of Carolina* (1996). Anjelica Huston, director. Starring Jena Malone, Ron Eldard, and Jennifer Jason Leigh.

Reading Icons:

Title: *The Best American Short Stories 1993*
Editor: Louise Erdrich
Genre: Short Stories **Number of Pages:** 395 **Date:** 1993
Level of Challenge: 4
Synopsis:
Every year, hundreds of short stories are published in literary magazines like *Harper's, Antaeus, The Paris Review,* and *The New Yorker.* At the end of the year, several anthologies of short fiction are edited from these sources; *The Best American Short Stories* is one of the most admired of these compilations, and the group of stories selected in 1993 was unusually impressive. The quotations below are taken from different stories in the anthology and are followed by the names of their authors in parenthesis.

Quotations:
"Vomiting, of course, was perennially big: the Technicolor yawn, riding the porcelain bus, talking to Ralph on the big white phone." (Jane Shapiro) Page 100.

"It's a place where a crooked TV preacher can pray that his flock will send him money so that he can build a giant water slide—and they will." (Tony Earley) Page 152.

"Prolonging anticipation—it's a very selfish taste I have. But without these little devices, I'll be honest with you, things get monotonous too quickly." (Andrea Lee) Page 209.

"He was a man distracted by his ignorance, acutely aware of the limits of his knowledge and therefore superior, in his own opinion, to his ignorant and complacent neighbors." (Joanna Scott) Page 217.

"I am not fond of travel in the best of circumstances—inconvenient displacements punctuated by painful longings to be home. For J., travel is natural opium." (Diane Johnson) Page 281.

Reading Hints:
Few readers can afford to subscribe to all the publications that publish good fiction, so anthologies like this are an excellent source of truly contemporary reading. There are twenty short stories in this anthology, and also a useful appendix naming "100 Other Distinguished Stories of 1992."

Reading Icons:

Title: *Blade Runner (Do Androids Dream of Electric Sheep?)*
Author: Philip K. Dick
Genre: Science Fiction **Number of Pages:** 216 **Date:** 1968

Level of Challenge: 2
Synopsis:
In the year 2021, after the World War Terminus, Rick Deckard, Bounty Hunter for the San Francisco Police, has to "retire" six rogue androids returned illegally from Mars. It's not as easy as it sounds, especially when some of the new generation of androids don't even know they are not human.
Quotations:
"Emigrate or degenerate! The choice is yours!" Page 6.
"Empathy, evidently, existed only within the human community, whereas intelligence to some degree could be found throughout every phylum and order including the arachnida." Page 26.
"Kipple is useless objects, like junk mail or match folders after you use the last match or gum wrappers or yesterday's homeopape. When nobody's around, kipple reproduces itself." Page 57.
Reading Hints:
It is interesting to compare Dick's novel with the movie *Blade Runner.* Each is excellent in its own way. Readers may want to ask themselves, however, why the departures from the original text were made by the filmmakers. Philip K. Dick is a writer of strong ideas, some of them perhaps too strong for Hollywood.
Others by Dick: *We Can Remember It for You Wholesale* (science fiction), *The Simulacra* (science fiction), and *The Collected Stories of Philip K. Dick: The Minority Report* (science fiction).
Movie: *Blade Runner* (1982). Ridley Scott, director. Starring Harrison Ford, Rutger Hauer, and Sean Young.

Reading Icons:

Title: *The Body Farm*
Author: Patricia Cornwell
Genre: Mystery Novel **Number of Pages:** 351 **Date:** 1994
Level of Challenge: 2
Synopsis:
Dr. Kay Scarpetta—forensic pathologist, lawyer, and medical doctor—is confronted with two perplexing mysteries in *The Body Farm.* The first is the brutal murder of eleven-year-old Emily Steiner; the second is the apparent dishonesty of her favorite niece and FBI trainee, Lucy. Juggling both conundrums simultaneously, Dr. Scarpetta shows uncanny technical ability, impressive intuition, and understandable human frailty.

Quotations:

"My frustration grew as he continued to talk. I wondered what had been missed. I wondered what microscopic witnesses had been silenced forever." Pages 27–28.

"Computers were the modern Babel, I had decided. The higher technology reached, the greater the confusion of tongues." Page 35.

"To almost die is to know that one day you will, and to never again feel the same about anything." Page 197.

"No one respects the dead more than those of us who work with them and hear their silent stories. The purpose is to help the living." Page 277.

Reading Hints:

The classic mystery novel has a long and illustrious history, including suspenseful stories by Edgar Allen Poe, Arthur Conan Doyle, and Agatha Christie. Interestingly, as the methods of law enforcement have gotten significantly more sophisticated in the twenty-first century, the current mystery novel has kept pace by becoming much more technical. Dr. Scarpetta is the Sherlock Holmes of the modern age, relying more on brains than brawn to bring terrible criminals to justice.

Others by Cornwell: *Body of Evidence* (novel), *All That Remains* (novel), and *Postmortem* (novel).

Reading Icons:

Title: *The Bomb and the General*
Author: Umberto Eco and Eugenio Carmi (illustrator)
Genre: Children's Book **Number of Pages:** 40 **Date:** 1989
Level of Challenge: 1 (Reading Ages 4–8)
Synopsis:

The Bomb and the General introduces children to atoms, bombs, generals, and the idea of war. It also leaves a strong impression that nothing loves a bomb, not even the atoms that make it up. This ambitious children's book was written by Italian novelist and scholar Umberto Eco, translated into English by William Weaver, and illustrated with Windsor and Newton watercolors and collage by Eugenio Carmi.

Quotations:

"Once upon a time there was an atom." Page 1.

"Well, our atom was sad because it had been put inside an atomic bomb." Page 10.

"And so the atoms decided to rebel against the general." Page 16.

Reading Hints:
This is a wonderful story that readers may want to share with their children. It's important to realize that in books like *The Bomb and the General,* the illustrations are as important as the text. For example, on page 17 there is a beautiful picture of the atoms abandoning their bombs and becoming an intricate lacelike pattern on a woman's blouse. Lingering over the illustrations is part of the joy of reading really good children's books.

Others by Eco: *The Name of the Rose* (novel), *Foucault's Pendulum* (novel), and *Baudolino* (novel).

Reading Icons:

Title: *A Box of Matches*
Author: Nicholson Baker
Genre: Novel **Number of Pages:** 178 **Date:** 2003
Level of Challenge: 4
Synopsis:
Emmett is a forty-four-year-old man, an editor of medical textbooks, married with children, cats, and a duck. He embarks, in January at 4:17 AM, on a new regime of getting up early before the rest of his household, lighting a fire, having a cup of coffee, and taking the time to think. His ruminations encompass one-match fires, the human yawn, the sound of train horns, the cause of dreams, belly button lint, paper towel designs, and so much more. Is the meaning of life hidden in such minutia—perhaps?
Quotations:
"I would like to visit the factory that makes train horns, and ask them how they are able to arrive at that chord of eternal mournfulness. Is it deliberately sad?" Page 22.

"I knew that we would remember this moment better than other perhaps worthier or more representative moments because we were taking pictures of it." Page 37.

"Marines, so Ronnie told me, generally want their hair mown shorter than any other group of military men. They want to look like penile tubes of warmongeringness." Page 57.

"Isn't it pleasing when you ask a question of a person, a teacher, or a speaker, and he or she says, That's a good question? Don't you feel good when that happens?" Page 175.

Reading Hints:
The older a work of literature is, the more likely it will be about kings and queens, or other characters of considerable stature. Modern literature is more interested in ordinary folks, sometimes put in extraordinary situations. An even more contemporary trend in fiction is to restrict the action of the plot to a single day, or in this case, to the predawn moments of an early morning fire. Our contemporary writers seem to be asking the question, "how much meaning can be eked out of the smallest detail or circumstance?"
Others by Baker: *Room Temperature* (novel), *The Mezzanine* (novel), and *Vox* (novel).

Reading Icons:

Title: *Brave New World*
Author: Aldous Huxley
Genre: Novel **Number of Pages:** 177 **Date:** 1932
Level of Challenge: 3
Synopsis:
Everyone is happy in Huxley's Brave New World. Old age, serious illness, unemployment, even discontent are almost entirely eliminated. Every modern form of recreation is readily available, including sex and the wonder drug Soma. So why isn't Bernard Marx happy? What happened to art and science and beauty? And can Shakespeare and "The Savage" teach civilized man anything worth knowing? In a superficially benign utopia, over five hundred years in the future, Huxley ponders these questions and more.
Quotations:
"That is the secret of happiness and virtue—liking what you've got to do. All conditioning aims at that: making people like their unescapable social destiny." Page 10.
"Why was that old fellow [Shakespeare] such a marvelous propaganda technician? Because he had so many insane, excruciating things to get excited about. You've got to be hurt and upset; otherwise, you can't think of the really good, penetrating, X-rayish phrases." Page 125.
"Actual happiness always looks pretty squalid in comparison with the overcompensations for misery. And of, course, stability isn't nearly so spectacular as instability. And being contented has none of the glamour of a good fight against misfortune, none of the picturesqueness of a struggle with temptation, or a fatal overthrow by passion or doubt. Happiness is never grand." Page 150.

Reading Hints:
Often modern authors make reference to prior pieces of literature, or moments in history, or mythological characters—these references are called *allusions*. The title of Huxley's novel is an allusion to lines in Shakespeare's play *The Tempest*. In fact, throughout the novel, Huxley quotes Shakespeare without attribution, assuming that everyone will know the master's words. Readers might like to see how many allusions to Shakespeare's writing they can find in *Brave New World* (Hint: pay attention to the dialog of The Savage).
Others by Huxley: *Brave New World Revisited* (essays) and *Chrome Yellow* (novel).
Movie: *Brave New World* (1998 TV). Leslie Libman, director. Starring Tim Guinee, Sally Kirkland, and Peter Gallagher.

Reading Icons:

Title: *The Catcher in the Rye*
Author: J. D. Salinger
Genre: Novel **Number of Pages:** 214 **Date:** 1951
Level of Challenge: 4
Synopsis:
Catcher in the Rye is the classic coming-of-age story, written by a young man recovering from a breakdown after being thrown out of prep school. He writes about wandering around Manhattan for a lost weekend, drinking too much, calling up old classmates and teachers, befriending a couple of nuns, sneaking in to see his beloved sister, and trying to make some sense of his disheveled life.
Quotations:
"This is about the fourth school I've gone to. . . . Partly because I have a lousy vocabulary and partly because I act quite young for my age sometimes." Page 8.
"I can never get really sexy—I mean really sexy—with a girl I don't like a lot. . . . Boy, it really screws up my sex life something awful. My sex life stinks." Page 148.
"I'd have this rule that nobody could do anything phony when they visited me. If anybody tried to do anything phony, they couldn't stay." Page 205.
Reading Hints:
Although by modern standards *Catcher in the Rye* is quite a tame book, it is still the most banned book in America. Readers might like to consider what

was so upsetting to people in the 1950s about this book, and what still bothers some people today.

Others by Salinger: *Franny and Zooey* (novel), *Nine Stories* (short stories).

Reading Icons:

Title: *The Color Purple*
Author: Alice Walker
Genre: Novel **Number of Pages:** 295 **Date:** 1982
Level of Challenge: 4
Synopsis:
The Color Purple is an unsentimental and powerful look at the lives of a loosely connected "family" of blacks living in pre–civil rights America. Celie, tragically used as a young girl, finds her own way to independence through her letters to God; her enduring love for her runaway sister and missing children; her wise and fierce women friends; her nurturing lover; and her own indomitable strength and common sense.

Quotations:
"He beat me today cause he say I winked at a boy in the church. I may have got something in my eye but I didn't wink. I don't even look at mens. That's the truth." Page 6.

"That when I notice how Shug talk and act sometimes like a man. Men say stuff like that to women, Girl, you look like a good time. Women always talk bout hair and health. How many babies living or dead, or got teef." Page 85.

"I remember one time you said your life made you feel so ashamed you couldn't even talk about it to God, you had to write it, bad as you thought your writing was." Page 136.

"The thing I believe. God is inside you and inside everybody else. You come into the world with God. But only them that search for it inside find it." Page 202.

Reading Hints:
Many readers expect all novels to be written in standard English, but some talented writers are able to let their characters speak in their own authentic voices. Alice Walker has a remarkable ear for dialect, and Celie, Shug, Nettie, and the other characters in her novel, all speak like real individuals with varying degrees of education and different life experiences. Don't worry too much about grammar and spelling, just enjoy the natural rhythms of this southern black speech, the language of the blues.

Others by Walker: *Possessing the Secret of Joy* (novel), *The Same River Twice* (novel), and *Meridian* (novel).
Movie: *The Color Purple* (1985). Steven Spielberg, director. Starring Danny Glover, Whoopi Goldberg, and Oprah Winfrey.

Reading Icons:

Title: *The Corrections*
Author: Jonathan Franzen
Genre: Novel **Number of Pages:** 567 **Date:** 2001
Level of Challenge: 4
Synopsis:
This is the story of the Lamberts: Enid, whose life's ambition is to get her entire family back home for one last old-fashioned Christmas; Alfred, her husband, whose Parkinson's disease has put him in a less than festive mood; and Gary, Chip, and Denise, the grown children, who have late-twentieth-century problems of their own. The values and traditions of the American Midwest have rarely been so thoroughly skewered and so lovingly cherished in a single book.
Quotations:
"It galled him that romantics like Enid could not distinguish the false from the authentic; a poor-quality, flimsily stocked, profit making 'museum' from a real, honest railroad." Page 258.
"What you discovered about yourself in raising children wasn't always agreeable or attractive." Page 263.
"Apparently she had that ability of the enviable, of the non-midwestern, of the moneyed, to assess her desires without regard to social expectations or moral imperatives." Page 314.
"She had a thing for a straight woman who was married to a man whom she herself might have liked to marry. It was a reasonably hopeless case." Page 409.
Reading Hints:
Very early in the book there is a single sentence of interior monologue that is a full page long. It is a model of how really long sentences can be written and controlled, but it still might cause the reader some difficulty. Remember that it is not at all unusual for the reader to be somewhat confused when taken directly into the mind of a man suffering from Parkinson's disease who is in a moment of confusion himself.
Others by Franzen: *The Twenty-Seventh City* (novel), *Strong Motion* (novel).

Reading Icons:

Title: *Crime and Punishment*
Author: Fyodor Dostoyevsky
Genre: Novel **Number of Pages:** 542 **Date:** 1866
Level of Challenge: 5
Synopsis:
Raskolnikov, a young, arrogant, intellectual is fascinated by Napoleon's idea that certain special men are not bound by civil law like their less remarkable fellow citizens. Such a man might rob or kill with impunity and experience no psychological cost. Is Raskolnikov such a man? There is only one way to find out.
Quotations:
"There are some people who interest us immediately, at first glance, before a word is exchanged. The customer sitting by himself who looked like a retired government clerk had this effect on Raskolnikov." Page 21.

"While committing his crime, almost every criminal seemed subject to a failure of judgment and of the will, which gave way to a phenomenal, childish recklessness at the very moment when he needed caution and judgment the most." Page 78.

"I believe that if circumstances prevented the discovery of a Kepler or Newton from becoming known except through the sacrifice of a man's life, or of ten, or a hundred, or as many as you please, who prevented this discovery or blocked its path as an obstacle, Newton would have the right, he would even be obligated . . . to remove these ten men, or these hundred men, so he could make his discoveries known to all mankind." Page 257.

Reading Hints:
Many masterworks of literature embody a philosophy, the principles of which are worked out through the characters in the story. Often the author and the characters actually have different ideas. Raskolnikov's ideas are tested in this novel, but the reader will want to pay attention to Dostoyevsky's final judgment on the character of Raskolnikov and the consequences of his actions.

Others by Dostoyevsky: *The Idiot* (novel), *The Demons* (novel), and *The Brothers Karamazov* (play).

Movie: *Crime and Punishment* (1999). Joseph Sargent, director. Starring Patrick Dempsy, Ben Kingsley, and Julie Delpy.

Reading Icons:

Title: *Curious George*
Author: H. A. Rey
Genre: Children's Book **Number of Pages:** 56 **Date:** 1941
Level of Challenge: 1 (Reading Ages 3–8)
Synopsis:
This is the story of the little African monkey who was so curious that he ended up in a zoo. Along the way, he had many adventures, including a trip in a big ship, telephoning a fire department, spending the night in jail, and flying over the city hanging on to a colorful bunch of balloons. Constantly in danger of drowning, falling, or causing mischief, Curious George always manages to smile and survive his mishaps.
Quotations:
"The man with the big yellow hat/put George into a little boat. . . . George was sad, but he was still/a little curious." Page 12.
"And then he was lucky to be a monkey/out he walked on to the telephone wires." Page 42.
"He felt he *must* have/a bright red balloon." Page 44.
Reading Hints:
Curious George has such simple pictures and text that it is an excellent book to read to very young children. Even adult readers may be able to remember when they were fascinated by hats and telephones, firemen, and balloons.
Others by Rey: *Curious George Takes a Job* (children's book), *Curious George Learns the Alphabet* (children's book), and *See the Circus* (children's book).
Movie: *Curious George* (1991). Claymation. United American Video, featuring John Matthews.

Reading Icons:

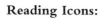

Title: *Dance upon the Air*
Author: Nora Roberts
Genre: Romance Novel **Number of Pages:** 386 **Date:** 2001
Level of Challenge: 2
Synopsis:
This is the first book in the Three Sisters Island trilogy. It has all the elements of a classic romance novel: Nell, the beleaguered heroine; Sheriff

Todd, the handsome young hero; Evan, the tyrannical husband; and Mia, the wise older woman, who just might also be a witch.

Quotations:

"For the first time in nine months, she began to plan for a future that included bank accounts, mail delivery, and personal possessions that couldn't be stuffed into a duffel or backpack at a moment's notice." Page 146.

"Shopping for shoes has nothing to do with need, and everything to do with lust." Page 147.

"Spells were, Nell decided, really just a kind of recipe. And there she was on solid ground. A recipe required time, care, and quality ingredients in proper proportions for success." Page 256.

"Laying a hand on his heart, she timed its beats to her own. And knew the truest magic was there." Page 373.

Reading Hints:

Romance novels are formula fiction, but many readers might be surprised how much the formula has changed in the last twenty years. *Dance upon the Air* has a historical element, but the novel is grounded firmly in the twenty-first century. The heroine is beleaguered but is not without courage or skills herself. The hero is manly but has a sensitive side. And the "witch" not only casts spells but uses a computer.

Others by Roberts: *Carolina Moon* (novel), *Heart of the Sea* (novel), and *The Villa* (novel).

Reading Icons:

Title: *Day of the Dead*
Author: Tony Johnston and Jeanette Winter (illustrator)
Genre: Children's Book **Number of Pages:** 42 **Date:** 1997
Level of Challenge: 1 (All Ages)
Synopsis:

This is the story of one small town in Mexico and how its citizens honor the spirits of their departed loved ones through singing, dancing, decorating with flowers, sharing stories, and having a wonderful feast. Spanish words are integrated into the English text so gracefully that both adult and young readers will have the impression that they are actually bilingual.

Quotations:

"Above a small town in Mexico,/the sun rises/like a great marigold." Page 1.

"For weeks the family/has been preparing for this day./*Los ti'os,* the uncles,
e picked fruit." Page 5.

"Upon the graves they leave the marigolds./Then they go walking, walking home, carrying candles like stars." Page 42.

Reading Hints:
Some cultures celebrate Halloween, some All Hallows' Eve, and some the Day of the Dead. All these observances in late October mark the beginning of fall, and most have traditions surrounding food, song, ghosts, and the macabre aspects of life and death. Reading a book with a theme like this one with children is a good way to check in on their thoughts about departed loved ones and the deaths they see on TV every day.

Others by Johnston: *That Summer* (children's book), *The Quilt Story* (children's book), and *The Cowboy and the Black-Eyed Pea* (children's book).

Reading Icons:

Title: *The Day of the Triffids*
Author: John Wyndham
Genre: Novel **Number of Pages:** 222 **Date:** 1951
Level of Challenge: 3
Synopsis:
Earth is showered with brilliant green meteors, and anyone who gazes at them is blinded, leaving the world with very few sighted people. What can, or should, the lucky ones do for the ones who are sightless? And what kind of an advantage might a suddenly blind humanity give to the mobile but congenitally blind Triffids? And where did the meteors, the plague, and the Triffids come from, anyway?

Quotations:
"The way I came to miss the end of the world—well, the end of the world I had known for close on thirty years–was sheer accident: like a lot of survival, when you come to think of it." Page 9.

"Do we help those who have survived the catastrophe to rebuild some kind of life? Or do we make a moral gesture which on the face of it, can scarcely be more than a gesture?" Page 87.

"I'm making no definite theory, but I do say this: they [the Triffids] took advantage of our disadvantages with remarkable speed. I also say that there is something perceptibly like method going on among them right now." Page 192.

Reading Hints:
Readers will notice that *The Day of the Triffids* was written in 1951, at the height of the hysteria of the Cold War between the United States and the

Soviet Union. Some thinkers, like Wyndham, were wondering what yet unimagined dangers the nuclear arms buildup and the continued global rivalry might engender. In the age of widespread terrorism, Wyndham seems particularly prophetic.

Others by Wyndham: *The Midwich Cuckoos* (novel), *Out of the Deeps* (novel), and *Re-Birth* (novel).

Movie: *The Day of the Triffids* (1962). Steve Sekely, director. Starring Howard Keel, Nicole Maurey, and Kieron Moore.

Reading Icons:

Title: *Despair*
Author: Vladimir Nabokov
Genre: Novel **Number of Pages:** 212 **Date:** 1965
Level of Challenge: 5
Synopsis:
This is the mystery of Hermann, a man determined to pull off the perfect crime. Along the way, the very unreliable narrator invites the reader to sample various literary styles, consider the peculiarity of twins and doubles, and experience the thinking of an unusually inventive madman.

Quotations:
"Two persons resembling each other do not present any interest when met singly, but create quite a stir when both appear at once." Page 79.
"If the deed is planned and performed correctly, then the force of creative art is such, that were the criminal to give himself up on the very next morning, none would believe him, the invention of art containing far more intrinsical truth than life's reality." Page 122.
"I never stole peaches from the hothouse. . . . I never buried cats alive. I never twisted the arms of playmates weaker than myself; but, as I say, I composed abstruse verse and elaborate stories, with dreadful finality and without any reason whatever lampooning acquaintances of my family." Page 45.

Reading Hints:
Some storytellers break right into the story and speak directly to the reader. These "intrusions" often contain vital information about the reliability of the narrator and the story he is telling. Hermann leaves a lot of clues that he might not be the most reliable person and that the reader might want to examine anything that he says pretty closely. (Example: "A slight digression: that bit about my mother was a deliberate lie." Page 4.)

Others by Nabokov: *Lolita* (novel), *Pale Fire* (novel), and *Nabokov's Dozen* (short stories).

Reading Icons:

Title: *Dr. Jekyll and Mr. Hyde*
Author: Robert Louis Stevenson
Genre: Gothic Novel **Number of Pages:** 103 **Date:** 1886
Level of Challenge: 2
Synopsis:
The respected Dr. Jekyll is involved in strange and secret experiments behind the locked doors of his laboratory. They have something to do with a loathsome stranger, Mr. Hyde, who is suddenly a questionable but important guest. Friends, servants, lawyers, the police, as well as readers, all try to solve the mystery at the center of this dark tale.
Quotations:
"Henry Jekyll became too fanciful for me. He began to go wrong, wrong in mind . . . unscientific balderdash." Page 12.
"Only on one point were they agreed; and that was the haunting sense of unexpressed deformity with which the fugitive impressed his beholders!" Page 32.
"Life would be relieved of all that was unbearable; the unjust might go his way, delivered from the aspirations and remorse of his more upright twin; and the just could walk steadfastly and securely on his upward path." Page 80.
Reading Hints:
Novels with very strange plots often try to authenticate their stories by using letters, documents, pronouncements, newspaper articles, and wills to make them seem more credible. Notice how many of these devices Stevenson uses in *Dr. Jekyll and Mr. Hyde.*
Others by Stevenson: *Treasure Island* (novel), *New Arabian Nights* (short stories), and *Weir of Hermiston* (novel).
Movies: *Dr. Jekyll and Mr. Hyde* (1921). John S. Robertson, director. Starring John Barrymore and Nita Naldi.
Dr. Jekyll and Mr. Hyde (1931). Rouben Mamoulian, director. Starring Fredric March and Miriam Hopkins.

Reading Icons:

Title: *Dracula*
Author: Bram Stoker
Genre: Novel **Number of Pages:** 327 **Date:** 1897
Level of Challenge: 4
Synopsis:
On one level, *Dracula* is the first successful vampire novel in English, and the best of them; on another level, it is a spellbinding mystery (will all the coffins be found?); and on still a third level, it is about human frailty and cooperation in the face of supernatural evil. Rich with vampire lore, nineteenth-century optimism about science, and psychological insight, this book has something for almost every reader.
Quotations:
"When I asked him if he knew Count Dracula and could tell me anything of his castle, both he and his wife crossed themselves, and saying that they knew nothing at all, simply refused to speak further." Page 14.
"Let me tell you, my friend, that there are things done today in electrical science which would have been deemed unholy by the very men who discovered electricity—who would themselves not so long before have been burned as wizards. There are always mysteries in life." Page 197.
"Take the papers that are with this, the diaries of Harker and the rest, and read them, and then find this great Un-Dead, and cut off his head and burn his heart or drive a stake through it, so that the world may rest from him." Page 209.
Reading Hints:
Vampires are well known characters in the twenty-first century, but they were exotic imports from Eastern Europe in Stoker's nineteenth century. Try to imagine what it would be like to be reading about such creatures for the first time.
Others by Stoker: *The Lair of the White Worm* (novel), "The Judge's House" (short story), and *The Lady of the Shroud* (novel).
Movies: *Nosferatu* (1921). F. W. Murnau, director. Starring Max Schreck, Gustav von Wangenheim, and Greta Schroder.
Dracula (1931). Tod Browning, director. Starring Bela Lugosi, Helen Chandler, and David Manners.
Dracula (1958). Terence Fisher, director. Starring Peter Cushing, Christopher Lee, and Melissa Stribling
Bram Stoker's Dracula (1992). Francis Ford Coppola, director. Starring Gary Oldman, Winona Rider, and Anthony Hopkins.

Reading Icons:

Title: *The Dying Animal*
Author: Philip Roth
Genre: Novel **Number of Pages:** 156 **Date:** 2001
Level of Challenge: 4
Synopsis:
David Kepesh, professor and cultural critic, has lived a life of epicurean delight, dallying with his promising young female students. He keeps a safe emotional distance, that is, until Consuela Castillo, demure, and astoundingly attractive, walks into his classroom and forever changes the trajectory of his orderly, but perhaps slightly sterile, life.
Quotations:
"A good heart, a lovely face, a gaze at once inviting and removed, gorgeous breasts, and so newly hatched as a woman that to find fragments of broken shell adhering to that ovoid forehead wouldn't have been a surprise. I saw right away that this was going to be my girl." Page 5.
"No matter how much you know, no matter how much you think, no matter how much you plot and you connive and you plan, you're not superior to sex. It's a very risky game." Page 33.
"Kenny was one of those overheated kids for whom whatever he read had a personal significance that eradicated everything else germane to literature." Page 78.
Reading Hints:
Readers will note that Dr. Kepesh's ideas about sexuality are a reasoned version of the ideas prevalent in the 1960s in liberated America. Readers may want to examine their own thoughts about sexuality and see how they hold up, both in relation to Dr. Kepesh's ideas and to their own subsequent experiences.
Others by Roth: *American Pastoral* (novel), *Goodbye, Columbus* (novel), and *The Professor of Desire* (novel).

Reading Icons: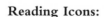

Title: *Elmer Gantry*
Author: Sinclair Lewis

Genre: Novel **Number of Pages:** 416 **Date:** 1927
Level of Challenge: 3
Synopsis:
Sinclair Lewis explores the state of religion in America after the turn of the twentieth century by chronicling the rise of Elmer Gantry from itinerant preacher to tent evangelist, to head of the fundamentalist Christian movement. Fond of wine, women, and song, Gantry is a lively American clergyman, as full of ambition as of spiritual fire.

Quotations:
"He never said anything important, and he always said it sonorously. He could make 'good morning' seem profound as Kant, welcoming as a brass band, and uplifting as a cathedral organ." Page 9.

"Of one duty he was never weary; of standing around and being impressive and very male for the benefit of lady seekers." Page 188.

"You see, Phil, I was brought up to believe the Christian God wasn't a scared and compromising public servant, but the creator and advocate of the whole merciless truth, and I reckon that training spoiled me—I actually took my teachers seriously!" Page 357.

"How preachers did talk! Did plasterers and authors and stockbrokers sit up half the night discussing their souls, fretting as to whether plastering or authorship or stockbroking was worth while?" Page 360.

Reading Hints:
Satire is the use of humor, irony, or ridicule to expose vices and critique the status quo. Most satirists are disgruntled idealists, and Sinclair Lewis is no exception. Irony sometimes causes readers to misunderstand authors, because the characters in a novel often espouse views with which the authors may not agree. For example, it's important to remember that the sentiment expressed by a workman watching a female evangelist in *Elmer Gantry* ("Woman's all right in her place, but it takes a real he-male to figure out this religion business") belongs to the workman, not to the author Sinclair Lewis.

Others by Lewis: *Babbitt* (novel), *Main Street* (novel), and *Arrowsmith* (novel).

Movie: *Elmer Gantry* (1960). Richard Brooks, director. Starring Burt Lancaster, Shirley Jones, and Jean Simmons.

Reading Icons:

Title: *Even Cowgirls Get the Blues*
Author: Tom Robbins

Genre: Novel **Number of Pages:** 365 **Date:** 1976
Level of Challenge: 4
Synopsis:
Sissy Hankshaw was born with enormous thumbs, so she felt sure she was destined to be a hitchhiker. Her many road trips take her to a radically feminist ranch, an American Indian husband, a modeling career, and a last-ditch effort to save the whooping cranes.
Quotations:
"Sissy never really dreamed of hitching to anywhere; it was the act of hitching that formed the substance of her vision." Page 23.
"It is questionable, for that matter, whether success is an adequate response to life. Success can eliminate as many options as failure." Page 10.
"The whooping crane practiced the science of the particular; it enacted the singular as opposed to the general; it embodied the exception rather than the rule." Page 251.
"This author's advice to his readers is to make the best you can of your brain—it's pretty good storage space and the price is right—and then turn to something else." Page 141.
Reading Hints:
This novel is meant to be appreciated at the sentence level. Robbins's first love is language. Don't rush your reading, and don't expect the plot to be realistic or even probable.
Others by Robbins: *Another Roadside Attraction* (novel), *Fierce Invalids Home from Hot Climates* (novel), and *Still Life with Woodpecker* (novel).
Movie: *Even Cowgirls Get the Blues* (1993). Gus Van Sant, director. Starring Uma Thurman, Lorraine Bracco, and Keanu Reeves.

Reading Icons:

Title: *Fateless*
Author: Imre Kertész
Genre: Novel **Number of Pages:** 191 **Date:** 1975
Level of Challenge: 3
Synopsis:
George Koves is a Jewish Hungarian teenager who finds himself a survivor of the German concentration camps of Auschwitz, Buchenwald, and Zeitz. On his return to Budapest, family and friends either want him to forget his recent experiences entirely or revel obscenely in their horrors. Neither mode suits him; instead, he wants to tell his story honestly in all its unbelievable

banality, and occasional beauty—a tale of naivety, boredom, confusion, and of a young mind trying to apply everyday logic to totally illogical events.

Quotations:

"I think that we should have been studying about Auschwitz all along, if they had tried to explain everything openly, honestly, intelligently. During the four years at school I did not hear a single word about this place. Still, of course, I realized that it would have been embarrassing, and I guess it really wasn't part of our general education." Page 83.

"This boredom, combined with this strange waiting, was, I think, approximately what Auschwitz meant to me, but of course I am only speaking for myself." Page 87.

"In all the people I noticed the same eagerness, the same good intentions. They too were determined to prove themselves to be model prisoners. No question about it: That was in our own self interest. That was what was required by the circumstances. That is what life, so to speak, demanded." Page 105.

"Yes, that's what I'll tell them the next time they ask me; about the happiness in those camps. If they ever do ask. And if I don't forget." Page 191.

Reading Hints:

Fateless is told by a fifteen-year-old boy of average intelligence and experience. As a narrator he has certain advantages (he is honest, observant, and dispassionate) and certain disadvantages (he is not very curious, he relies exclusively on logic, and he is understandably naïve about the world and human nature). The story of the Holocaust is a huge one, but each time a new narrative voice is presented to us, we understand its meaning a little more fully.

Another by Kertész: *Kaddish for a Child Not Born* (novel).

Reading Icons:

Title: *The Five Chinese Brothers*
Author: Claire Huchet Bishop and Kurt Wiese (illustrator)
Genre: Children's Book **Number of Pages:** 44 **Date:** 1938
Level of Challenge: 1 (Reading Ages 4–8)
Synopsis:

In this Chinese fairy tale are five brothers who look exactly alike; each, however, has a special ability. One could "swallow the sea," one had an "iron ," one could "stretch and stretch his legs," one "could not be burned," and the fifth could "hold his breath indefinitely." When the first brother gets into trouble for an accidental drowning, all the brothers work together to save him.

Quotations:

"Near the shore the First Chinese Brother gathered some fish while he kept holding the sea in his mouth." Page 14.

"He was arrested, put in prison, tried and condemned to have his head cut off." Page 23.

"We have tried to get rid of you in every possible way and somehow it cannot be done. It must be that you are innocent." Page 42.

Reading Hints:

It is very refreshing to read children's books that tell stories from other cultures. *The Five Chinese Brothers* tells a story familiar to Chinese children but that will be surprising to most Western readers. Children's books are an easy and pleasurable way for adult readers to learn mythology, biblical stories, and the beloved stories of the whole world. Themes like "succeeding through cooperation" turn up in the literatures of all places, at all times.

Others by Bishop: *Twenty and Ten* (children's book), *Christopher the Giant* (children's book), and *The Man Who Lost His Head* (children's book).

Reading Icons:

Title: *Flicker*

Author: Theodore Roszak

Genre: Novel **Number of Pages:** 588 **Date:** 1991

Level of Challenge: 3

Synopsis:

Theodore Roszak himself called this novel "a secret history of the movies." It follows the quest of film lover Jonathan Gates as he tries to unravel the strange disappearance of Max Castle, silent-screen genius turned film-noir director. Are movies just vehicles of simple entertainment or part of a centuries-old, international, quasi-religious plot?

Quotations:

"She insisted that movies were something more than a bag of optical illusions; they were literature for the eye, potentially as great as anything ever written for the page." Page 42.

"The flicker was how you made the tricks happen just right. First you had to get hold of the flicker, see? Then you could stick in all the tricks you wanted." Page 164.

"At the current rate of accelerating perceptual shrinkage, Julien predicted
    that the adolescent generation of the year 2000 would have no atten-
    tion span whatever, hence no capacity to absorb any message longer
    than a single cinematic flash frame in duration." Page 267.
"That's the theory we're working from. Bad is better than okay. Bad is best.
    Because bad opens up a space, you understand? It gives things a
    chance to grow." Page 339.

Reading Hints:

Flicker is an intelligent book about movies and American audiences; surprisingly, it has never been made into a Hollywood movie or an independent film. Readers might enjoy considering, as they read, how they might
cast and direct a movie made from this text.

Another by Roszak: *The Memoirs of Elizabeth Frankenstein* (novel).

Reading Icons:

Title: *forever peace*
Author: Joe Haldeman
Genre: Novel **Number of Pages:** 351 **Date:** 1997
Level of Challenge: 2
Synopsis:

In a future America, nanoforges supply all of people's actual needs, and lux-
uries are available to those who choose to work. War between the developed world and the third world has become even more lopsided, with
poorly equipped but passionate peasants on one side, fighting robotic "Sol-
dierboys," whose human operators are safe hundreds of miles away, on the
other. In the midst of all this controlled chaos, twenty old folks with con-
nections have a radical idea for peace.

Quotations:

"Mechanics aren't in any physical danger, deep inside the Operations
    bunker in Portobello. But our death and disability rate is higher than
    the regular infantry. It's not bullets that get us though; its our own
    brains and veins." Page 4.
"You could buy objects with money, like handcrafts and original art, or ser-
    vices; masseur, butler, prostitute. But most people spent money on ra-
    tional things—things the government allowed you to have, but didn't
    allow you enough of." Page 55.
"The people in his university life were mostly white but color blind, and
    the people he jacked with might have started out otherwise, but didn't

stay racist: you couldn't think black people were inferior if you lived inside black skin, ten days every month." Page 75.

Reading Hints:
Haldeman's major concern in this novel is the relationship of human nature to war and peace, but like all great science fiction writers, he fills his imaginary future with intriguing prophecies that could be jumping-off points for hundreds of other science fiction stories. For example: the anti-microwave, which cools things down rather than heats things up; the neutral expressions that people of the future adopt on picture-phones; the "resumption" of routine civilian space flight; and giant spiders that spin "silk" so strong that it has industrial applications.

Others by Haldeman: *The Forever War* (novel), *Forever Free* (novel), and *Worlds* (novel).

Reading Icons:

Title: *Frankenstein*
Author: Mary Shelley
Genre: Gothic Novel **Number of Pages:** 211 **Date:** 1818
Level of Challenge: 4
Synopsis:
Victor Frankenstein (the scientist) has created a "monster" from body parts of dead men and has animated it, brought it to life. This creature, which speaks fluent French and yearns for a mate, is abandoned at "birth" and wreaks havoc on his prideful creator. The novel addresses serious questions of parental, scientific, and moral responsibility that have plagued humans for generations.

Quotations:
"After days and nights of incredible labour and fatigue, I succeeded in discovering the cause of generation and life; nay, more I became myself capable of bestowing animation upon lifeless matter." Page 51.

"All men hate the wretched; how, then must I be hated, who am miserable beyond all living things? Yet you, my creator, detest and spurn me, thy creature, to whom thou art bound by ties only dissoluble by the annihilation of one of us." Page 95.

"None but those who have experienced them can conceive of the enticements of science. In other studies you go as far as others have gone before you, and there is nothing more to know; but in a scientific pursuit there is continual food for discovery and wonder." Page 49.

Reading Hints:
No other text in *Book Savvy* has had more movies made from it, and no other book shows more clearly how the movies interpret novels for their own purposes. James Whale's film (excellent in its own way) has a theme precisely the opposite of Mary Shelley's novel. Kenneth Branagh's film comes closest to being true to the novel, but it is also overwhelmed with special effects. It is always interesting to compare an original text with the artistic uses others make of it.
Others by Shelley: *Valperga* (novel), *The Last Man* (novel), and *Falkner* (novel).
Movies: *Frankenstein* (1931). James Whale, director. Starring Boris Karloff, Colin Clive, and Mae Clarke.
Mary Shelley's Frankenstein (1994) Kenneth Branagh, director. Starring Robert DeNiro, Kenneth Branagh, and Helena Bonham Carter.

Reading Icons:

Title: *Gaudy Night*
Author: Dorothy L. Sayers
Genre: Novel **Number of Pages:** 501 **Date:** 1936
Level of Challenge: 3
Synopsis:
Harriet Vane returns to her alma mater Oxford University for a reunion known as a "Gaudy Night" in 1935, only to be thrust into a perplexing mystery. Who is going about the staid women's college of Shrewsbury sending threatening letters, scrawling obscenities on the library walls, and upsetting dons (faculty members) and students alike? Lord Peter Wimsey, the perfect English gentleman and amateur sleuth, lends a helping hand with the solution to the mystery, as well as some romantic suspense to the story, as vexing questions of men's and women's roles in society are hotly and earnestly debated in the Seniors Common Room.
Quotations:
"To be true to one's calling, whatever follies one might commit in one's emotional life, that was the way to spiritual peace." Page 29.
"She admired the strange nexus of interests that unites the male half of mankind into a close honeycomb of cells, each touching the other on one side only, and yet constituting a tough and closely adhering fabric." Page 240.
"For good or evil, she had called in something explosive from the outside world to break up the ordered tranquility of the place; she had sold

the breach to an alien force; she had sided with London against Oxford and with the world against the cloister." Page 305.

"With tobacco and literature one could face out any situation, provided, of course, that the book was not written in an unknown tongue." Page 328.

Reading Hints:
Dorothy Sayers is a noted Christian scholar as well as a famous writer of detective stories. This academic side shows in her use of epigraphs from well-known authors at the beginning of each chapter in *Gaudy Night*. Readers need not be alarmed at the fact that some of the passages are poetry, or in Greek; there is always enough written in plain English to give a whopping clue as to what is going to occur later in that chapter.

Others by Sayers: *Strong Poison* (novel), *Have His Carcass* (novel), and *The Unpleasantness at the Bellona Club* (novel).

Movie: *Gaudy Night* (1987). BBC Adaptation. Starring Edward Petherbridge, Harriet Walter, and Merelina Kendall.

Reading Icons:

Title: *Hamlet, Prince of Denmark*
Author: William Shakespeare
Genre: Play Script **Number of Pages:** 46 **Date:** c. 1599
Level of Challenge: 5
Synopsis:
Did Hamlet's uncle Claudius kill his father, marry his mother, and usurp his throne? That's what the ghost, resembling Hamlet's father, says. Is it a good ghost unveiling a great wrong, or an evil spirit trying to lead Hamlet astray? A fearful mystery unravels as Hamlet tries to come to terms with his father's death, his mother's hasty remarriage, his lover's suicide, and his own grave misgivings.

Quotations:
"Frailty, thy name is woman!" Page 1078.
"Neither a borrower nor a lender be." Page 1080.
"Brevity is the soul of wit." Page 1088.
"What a piece of work is man!" Page 1090.
"To be, or not to be, that is the question." Page 1094.

Reading Hints:
Shakespeare is the most often quoted writer in the English language. In *Hamlet* alone readers will recognize dozens of lines even if they have never

read or seen the play before. Readers will want to note how their under-standing of these familiar quotations changes with their knowledge of the play as a whole.

Others by Shakespeare: *Othello* (play), *Macbeth* (play), and *The Taming of the Shrew* (play).

Movies: *Hamlet* (1948). Laurence Olivier, director. Starring Laurence Olivier, Eileen Herlie, and Basil Sydney.

Hamlet (1969). Tony Richardson, director. Starring Nicol Williamson, Anthony Hopkins, and Judy Parfitt.

Hamlet (1996). Kenneth Branagh, director. Starring Kenneth Branagh, Derek Jacobi, and Julie Christie.

Reading Icons:

Title: *Harry Potter and the Sorcerer's Stone*
Author: J. K. Rowling
Genre: Children's Novel **Number of Pages:** 309 **Date:** 1998
Level of Challenge: 1
Synopsis:
Catapulted from a hellish existence as the nephew of terribly normal Mr. and Mrs. Dursley to the prize student at Hogwart's School of Wizardry, Harry Potter, with his fellow students, the bookish Hermione Granger and the selfless Ron Weasley, show how cooperation can overcome incredible odds on the Quidditch field or in the search for the Sorcerer's Stone.

Quotations:
"'A Muggle,' said Hagrid, 'it's what we call nonmagic folk like them. An' it's your bad luck you grew up in a family o' the biggest Muggles I ever laid eyes on.'" Page 53.

"The four houses are called Gryffindor, Hufflepuff, Ravenclaw, and Slytherin. Each house has its own noble history and each has produced outstanding witches and wizards." Page 114.

"There are some things you can't share without ending up liking each other, and knocking out a twelve-foot mountain troll is one of them." Page 179.

Reading Hints:
Some readers are lucky enough to remember magical moments when their parents or grandparents read them stories aloud in the evening or on rainy days. All readers, whether they had those special experiences or not, now have the wonderful opportunity to share such moments with their children,

the kids on their block, or any underprivileged kids in their area who need a grown-up friend. Kids' books are best when shared with kids.

Others by Rowling: *Harry Potter and the Chamber of Secrets* (novel), *Harry Potter and the Goblet of Fire* (novel), and *Harry Potter and the Prisoner of Azkaban* (novel).

Movie: *Harry Potter and the Sorcerer's Stone* (2001). Chris Columbus, director. Starring Daniel Radcliffe and Rupert Grint.

Reading Icons:

Title: *Homebody/Kabul*
Author: Tony Kushner
Genre: Play Script **Number of Pages:** 151 **Date:** 2002
Level of Challenge: 5
Synopsis:
The playwright, Tony Kushner, sums up his play best in the "Afterword": "*Homebody/Kabul* is a play about Afghanistan and the West's historic and contemporary relationship to that country. It is also a play about travel, about knowledge and learning through seeking out strangeness, about trying to escape the unhappiness of one's [sic] life through an encounter with Otherness, about narcissism and self-referentiality as inescapable booby traps in any such encounter." It is one of those rare plays that is nearly as enjoyable to read as it is to see performed.

Quotations:
"My reading, my research is moth-like. Impassioned, fluttery, doomed." Page 9.
"You love the Taliban so much, bring them to New York! Well, don't worry, they're coming to New York! Americans!" Page 83.
"I am a poet, it is not possible that I lie." Page 92.
"A garden shows us what may await us in Paradise." Page 139.

Reading Hints:
The "Homebody's" language is intentionally dense, obscure, and sometimes irritating. Don't try to understand everything she says. Just let her words wash over you and keep an eye on the plot.

Others by Kushner: *Angels in America* (play), *Slavs!* (play), and *Hydriotaphia* (play).

Reading Icons:

Title: *Horseman, Pass By*
Author: Larry McMurtry
Genre: Western Novel **Number of Pages:** 179 **Date:** 1961
Level of Challenge: 3
Synopsis:
Horseman, Pass By is a western, a young cowboy's coming-of-age story, and
a painful look at the end of an important part of America's cultural history.
Lonnie, caught between the stalwart dignity of his rancher grandfather and
the charismatic, angry, hedonism of his fellow cowboy Scott; tries to find a
place for himself in the new and rapidly changing American West. This
novel provides a remarkably detailed and realistic description of ranching
life in mid-America around the 1950s.
Quotations:
"I could see Granddad in my mind a thousand ways, but always he was on
　　the ranch doing something. . . . I could see him riding, enjoying his
　　good horses: or I could see him tending the cattle; or see him just
　　standing in the grass, looking at the land and trying to figure out ways
　　to beat the dry weather and the wind." Page 167.
"In my grade-school days we had hung carcasses in the smokehouse, beeves
　　and hogs that Granddad and the cowboys butchered on frosty morn-
　　ings in November. . . . But now the beeves and hogs were in the locker
　　plant in Thalia, and the smokehouse only held broken lawn mowers
　　and spades and pieces of harness." Page 22.
"It had for me the good, special flavor of something seasonal, something you
　　have waited all winter to taste, like early roasting ears or garden toma-
　　toes." Page 7.
Reading Hints:
Western novels frequently return to certain basic themes. In this novel there
is the conflict between cow ranchers and oilmen, between settling down or
living the maverick life, and between city and country lifestyles. Some western novels, like *Horseman, Pass By,* transcend the western formula and are as
unpredictable and well written as any mainstream novel.
Others by McMurtry: *Lonesome Dove* (novel), *Terms of Endearment* (novel),
and *The Last Picture Show* (novel).
Movie: *Hud* (1963). Martin Ritt, director. Starring Paul Newman, Patricia
Neal, and Melvyn Douglas.

Reading Icons:

Title: *The Hours*
Author: Michael Cunningham
Genre: Novel **Number of Pages:** 226 **Date:** 1998
Level of Challenge: 4
Synopsis:
Cunningham has managed to interweave masterfully the lives of three un-
likely women: Virginia Woolf, during her final years of life in England in
1923–1941; Laura Brown, living the "American Dream" in Los Angeles in
1949; and Clarissa Vaughn, a bourgeois gay woman giving a celebratory
party for an artist who had immortalized her in his award-winning novel.
The book that binds them all together is *Mrs. Dalloway*—written by Virginia
Woolf, read with anguish by a trapped and confused Laura Brown; and re-
lived in a different era, and a completely unimagined way, by Clarissa
Vaughn.
Quotations:
"Tonight she will give her party. She will fill the rooms of her apartment
   with food and flowers, with people of wit and influence." Page 13.
"Not eating is a vice, a drug of sorts—with her stomach empty she feels
   quick and clean, clearheaded, ready for a fight." Page 34.
"In another world, she might have spent her whole life reading. But this is
   the new world, the rescued world—there's not much room for idle-
   ness." Page 39.
"But there are still the hours, aren't there? One and then another, and you
   get through that one and then, my god, there's another. I'm so sick."
   Page 198.
Reading Hints:
Some books are plotted in complicated and interesting patterns. Readers who
perceive the pattern quickly usually have no trouble reading the book, but
some readers have to read a book twice, with the ending in mind, to see how
cleverly the plot is constructed. Part of enjoying such books is appreciating the
intricate care with which they are put together. Other examples of unusually
patterned books are Homer's *Iliad* and Amy Tan's *The Joy Luck Club*.
Others by Cunningham: *A Home at the End of the World* (novel) and *Flesh
and Blood* (novel).
Movie: *The Hours* (2002), Stephen Daldry, director. Starring Meryl Streep,
Julianne Moore, and Nicole Kidman.

Reading Icons:

Title: *Household Saints*
Author: Francine Prose
Genre: Novel **Number of Pages:** 208 **Date:** 1981
Level of Challenge: 4
Synopsis:
Household Saints is the story of the Santangelo family, living in New York's Little Italy in the 1950s: Joseph, the crafty, loving butcher; Catherine, his wife, caught between old-country Italian ways and new American ones; and their daughter Teresa, the enigmatic household saint. On the surface a simple story of a simple family, *Household Saints* asks profound questions about tradition and modernity, organized religion and saintliness, and the power of love and commitment.

Quotations:
"For this was the way of the world, the facts of life, as natural and inevitable as gray hair; a man gets married, he stops playing pinochle. A few months later, the wife is pregnant and he's ready to play again." Page 70.

"For Catherine was bent on modeling herself after those women in the *Good Housekeeping* ads, those smiling, competent American housewives, their consciences as clear as their glassware." Page 102.

"Since then, she'd read dozens of saints' lives, preferring the ones who traveled and had adventures, like St. Helena, and the ones with the grisliest martyrdoms; she'd reread St. Lucy's blinding till she could hardy stand it. Most of all, though, she loved the saints who did crazy things, like St. Simon, perched atop a pillar in the desert for twenty years." Page 117.

"Maybe the burning bush was burning all the time and Moses didn't notice. Maybe the miracle is when you stop and pay attention." Page 202.

Reading Hints:
Household Saints is so light, engaging, and unassuming that it is easy for readers to fail to notice that it actually addresses some of the biggest questions of our time: What role does religion play in family life? How much of life is luck, and how much is conscious planning? Are miracles possible in the modern world? Are saints?

Others by Prose: *Animal Magnetism* (novel), *Bigfoot Dreams* (novel), and *Blue Angel* (novel).

Movie: *Household Saints* (1993). Nancy Savoca, director. Starring Tracey Ullman, Vincent D'Onofrio, and Lili Taylor.

Reading Icons:

Title: *The Hunchback of Notre Dame*
Author: Victor Hugo
Genre: Novel **Number of Pages:** 301 **Date:** 1831
Level of Challenge: 4
Synopsis:
Quasimodo, the deaf, deformed bell ringer of the Cathedral of Notre Dame, is the unlikely savior of La Esmeralda, the pagan gypsy dancer who is too beautiful for her own good. Set in a medieval Paris rife with political intrigue, rampant superstition, and strong passions, *Hunchback* is one of the greatest stories of loving heroism ever told.
Quotations:
"We shall do likewise and not attempt to give the reader an idea of that tetrahedron nose, that horseshoe mouth, that small left eye half hidden by a bristly red eyebrow while the right eye disappeared entirely behind an enormous wart, those irregular teeth jagged here and there like the battlements of a fortress, that horny lip over which one of those teeth protruded like an elephant's tusk, that forked chin and especially the expression spread over all this, that expression of mingled malice, amazement and sadness. Let the reader imagine it if he can." Page 15.
"The witchcraft of which the captain had been a victim seemed proved beyond the shadow of a doubt and in everyone's eyes La Esmeralda, that lovely dancer who had dazzled them so often with her grace, was now a horrifying witch." Page 159.
"Love is like a tree. It grows by itself, roots itself deeply in our being and continues to flourish over a heart in ruin. The inexplicable fact is that the blinder it is, the more tenacious it is. It is never stronger than when it is completely unreasonable." Page 205.
Reading Hints:
Every culture thinks differently about the relationship of beauty and ugliness to good and evil. Readers may want to track their own responses to excesses of beauty or ugliness, goodness or evil, knowledge or ignorance in the characters of this novel.
Others by Hugo: *Les Miserables* (play), *Selected Poems of Victor Hugo: A Bilingual Edition* (poems), and *The Toilers of the Sea* (novel).

Movies: *The Hunchback of Notre Dame* (1923). Wallace Worsley II, director. Starring Lon Chaney, Patsy Ruth Miller, and Norman Kerry.
The Hunchback of Notre Dame (1939). William Dieterle, director. Starring Charles Laughton, Cedric Hardwicke, and Maureen O'Hara.

Reading Icons:

Title: *If Beale Street Could Talk*
Author: James Baldwin
Genre: Novel **Number of Pages:** 166 **Date:** 1974
Level of Challenge: 4
Synopsis:
This is a love story about two young black people, Tish and Fonny, and their devoted families, who get caught up in the mean streets of racist New York in the 1970s. Poverty, crime, and drugs all play a part in the lives of these folks, who are barely surviving on the ragged edges of an inhospitable society. This is an unsentimental look at a painful place and time in America's history.

Quotations:
"They looked at us as though we were zebras—and, you know, some people like zebras and some people don't. But nobody ever asks the zebra." Page 8.

"I guess it can't be too often that two people can laugh and make love, too, make love because they are laughing, laugh because they're making love. The love and the laughter come from the same place: but not many people go there." Page 15.

"That same passion which saved Fonny got him into trouble, and put him in jail. For, you see, he had found his center, his own center, inside him: and it showed. He wasn't anybody's nigger." Page 32.

"For it is despair that Sharon is hearing, and despair, whether or not it can be taken home and placed on the family table, must always be respected. Despair can make one monstrous, but it can also make one noble." Page 126.

Reading Hints:
James Baldwin is a master writer of dialect, capturing, with a super-sensitive ear for meaning and nuance, the vocabulary and rhythms of nonstandard speakers of the English language. In *Beale Street* he records for all time the hip, edgy, sometimes obscene language of the impoverished streets, a language that would eventually work its way into the language of the middle

classes. He also tried to defuse the word "nigger," in the same way that D. H. Lawrence attempted to take the obscenity out of certain four-letter words. **Others by Baldwin:** *Giovanni's Room* (novel), *Another Country* (novel), and *The Fire Next Time* (novel).

Reading Icons:

Title: *Interpreter of Maladies*
Author: Jhumpa Lahiri
Genre: Short Stories **Number of Pages:** 198 **Date:** 1999
Level of Challenge: 4
Synopsis:
In nine deceptively quiet but powerful short stories, Lahiri shows how complicated life is, practically and emotionally, for recent Indian immigrants to America. Whether they came as expatriates of the partition, or hopeful merchants and entrepreneurs, or were born in America to immigrant parents, these newly minted citizens yearn for the mother country, India, and the old ways, even as they are inevitably seduced and transformed by their new American lives.
Quotations:
"At home . . . not everybody has a telephone. But just raise your voice a bit, or express grief or joy of any kind, and one whole neighborhood and half of another has come to share the news, to help with arrangements." Page 116.
"She was like that, excited and delighted by little things, crossing her fingers before any remotely unpredictable event, like tasting a new flavor of ice cream, or dropping a letter in a mailbox. It was a quality he did not understand. It made him feel stupid, as if the world contained hidden wonders he could not anticipate, or see." Page 142.
"For the greater number of her twenty-nine years, Bibi Haldar suffered from an ailment that baffled family, friends, priests, palmists, spinsters, gem therapists, prophets and fools." Page 158.
"We are American citizens now, so that we can collect social security when it is time. Though we visit Calcutta every few years, and bring back more drawstring pajamas and Darjeeling tea, we have decided to grow old here." Page 197.
Reading Hints:
Readers can learn a lot about their own culture by seeing it through "foreign" eyes. For example, contemporary Americans are fairly resigne

latchkey kids and older people spending their twilight years in convalescent homes, while such estrangements and alienations strike a deep chord of sadness in almost all of the Indian characters in Lahiri's stories.

Another by Lahiri: *The Namesake* (novel).

Reading Icons:

Title: *Interview with the Vampire*
Author: Anne Rice
Genre: Gothic Novel **Number of Pages:** 346 **Date:** 1976
Level of Challenge: 4
Synopsis:
In an interview, the vampire Louis tells the story of his life, from his early days as a Catholic youth living on a plantation to his conversion to vampirism by the powerful Lestat, to his quest for others of his kind across Eastern Europe to Paris. *Interview* takes a fascinating look at the nature of children, religion, good and evil, the erotic, and individual responsibility, while at the same time being a fast-paced, exciting vampire story.

Quotations:
"I'm not giving you what you want, am I? You wanted an interview. Something to broadcast on the radio." Page 67.

"They're jealous of their secret and of their territory; and if you find one or more of them together it will be for safety only, and one will be the slave of the other, the way you are of me!" Page 84.

"I remember that the movement of his lips raised the hair all over my body, sent a shock of sensation through my body that was not unlike the pleasure of passion." Page 18.

Reading Hints:
Readers who can suspend their disbelief long enough to imagine that vampires really exist can enjoy pondering all the questions posed by the possibility of eternal life, and wonder with the interviewer whether, if given a choice, they would choose the vampiric option.

Others by Rice: *The Witching Hour* (novel), *Feast of All Saints* (novel), and *The Queen of the Damned* (novel).

Movie: *Interview with the Vampire* (1994). Neil Jordan, director. Starring Tom Cruise, Brad Pitt, and Kirsten Dunst.

Reading Icons:

Title: *Jane Eyre*
Author: Charlotte Brontë
Genre: Novel **Number of Pages:** 456 **Date:** 1847
Level of Challenge: 5
Synopsis:
An orphan, a governess, and a woman of strong passions and integrity, Jane Eyre is the unlikely heroine of this highly romantic but strikingly unique love story. Right conduct, proper behavior, protofeminist ideas, and individual responsibility are all ingredients of a surprisingly modern and suspenseful mystery story.
Quotations:
"Children can feel, but they cannot analyze their feelings; and if the analysis is partially effected in thought, they know not how to express the result of the process in words." Page 26.
"You are aware that my plan in bringing up these girls is, not to accustom them to habits of luxury and indulgence, but to render them hardy, patient, self-denying." Page 65.
"Women are supposed to be very calm generally; but women feel just as men feel; they need exercise for their faculties, and a field for their efforts as much as their brothers do; they suffer from too rigid a constraint, too absolute a stagnation, precisely as men would suffer." Page 112.
Reading Hints:
In the nineteenth century, most women in England were expected to marry. Other outlets for their talents and imagination were very limited, particularly if they did not come from rich families. Try to empathize with the plight of a smart, plucky, sincere, young woman trying to find her way in such a time and society.
Others by Brontë: *Shirley* (novel), *Villette* (novel), and *The Professor* (novel).
Movies: *Jane Eyre* (1943). Robert Stevenson, director. Starring Joan Fontaine, Orson Welles, and Agnes Moorehead.
Jane Eyre (1970). Delbert Mann, director. Starring George C. Scott, Susannah York, and Ian Bannen.

Reading Icons:

Title: *The Joy Luck Club*
Author: Amy Tan
Genre: Novel **Number of Pages:** 288 **Date:** 1989

Level of Challenge: 4
Synopsis:
The Joy Luck Club fits together like an intricate Chinese box, showing both the complexity and the beauty of the lives of three immigrant Chinese mothers and their first generation Chinese-American daughters. As their histories and futures crisscross, a portrait of deep familial misunderstandings and even deeper love emerges. Clear-headed and yet passionate, this novel is rich in detail about the older China of the mothers and the newly diverse United States of the daughters.
Quotations:
"Each week, we could hope to be lucky. That hope was our only joy. And that's how we came to call our little parties Joy Luck." Page 25.

"My mother and I never really understood one another. We translated each other's meanings and I seemed to hear less than what was said, while my mother heard more." Page 37.

"A little knowledge withheld is a great advantage one should store for future use. That is the power of chess. It is a game of secrets, in which one must show and never tell." Page 95.

"They are fortunes. . . . American people think Chinese people write these sayings." Page 262.
Reading Hints:
Reading and travel are both ways of taking a journey. A book like *The Joy Luck Club* could easily inspire a reader to take a trip to San Francisco to see the sights in Chinatown there, or even to visit China and explore the magical caves of Guilin for themselves. Or a trip to San Francisco or China might encourage a reader to read *The Joy Luck Club,* so that he or she could more fully understanding the lives of the people in both of those places. Either way, reading and travel are natural companions.
Others by Tan: *The Bonesetter's Daughter* (novel), *The Kitchen God's Wife* (novel), and *The Hundred Secret Senses* (novel).
Movie: *The Joy Luck Club* (1993). Wayne Wang, director. Starring Ming-Na, Tamlin Tomita, and Rosalind Chao.

Reading Icons:

Title: *The Late George Apley*
Author: John P. Marquand
Genre: Novel **Number of Pages:** 402 **Date:** 1937
Level of Challenge: 4

Synopsis:

This *Novel in the Form of a Memoir* is the story of George Apley's life, commissioned by his son John and told by a friendly contemporary historian, using Apley's own papers, letters, and relatives as sources. It is a gentle social satire, assessing the life of a privileged, and yet oddly provincial, Bostonian gentleman who had lived through the remarkable changes that occurred in the United States between 1866 and 1933. At its heart, the novel explores the age-old human dilemma of whether moderation and stability, when all is said and done, trump a life of adventure and change.

Quotations:

"He once said of himself: 'I am the sort of man I am, because environment prevented my being anything else.'" Page 1.

"At no time in the history of the world have such material changes occurred as those in George Apleys' life span." Page 32.

"Distrust the book which reads too easily because such writing appeals more to the senses than to the intellect. Hard reading exercises the mind." Page 87.

"It sometimes seems to me that my father's generation did all there was to do, and left nothing to the rest of us." Page 168.

"One of the strangest phenomena of the last two decades was the illogical desire of many of the younger generation to escape physically from Boston." Page 295.

Reading Hints:

Marquand's novel is written in the form of a memoir. Many novels pretend to be something else. *Lolita* purports to be a statement to a jury; *Catcher in the Rye* is supposed to be a young boy's therapeutic journal; *Frankenstein* is written like a tale told to a ship's captain. It is interesting to think about what advantages a novelist is looking for when he casts his work in such a form.

Others by Marquand: *Thank You, Mr. Moto* (novel), *H. M. Pulham Esquire* (novel), and *So Little Time* (novel).

Reading Icons:

Title: *Lolita*
Author: Vladimir Nabokov
Genre: Novel **Number of Pages:** 288 **Date:** 1955
Level of Challenge: 5
Synopsis:
Nabokov has written a disturbing novel about a middle-aged European pedophile whose obsessive love for an underage girl damages a number of

lives, including his own. Told in the first person, by the child molester himself, this novel gives astonishing insight into the mind of a nearly unimaginable character.

Quotations:

"She was Lo, plain Lo, in the morning, standing four feet ten in one sock. She was Lola in slacks. She was Dolly at school. She was Dolores on the dotted line. But in my arms she was always Lolita." Page 11.

"Between the age limits of nine and fourteen there occur maidens who, to certain bewitched travelers, twice or many times older than they, reveal their true nature which is not human, but nymphic (that is, demoniac); and these chosen creatures I propose to designate as 'nymphets.'" Page 18.

"Despite my manly looks, I am horribly timid. My romantic soul gets all clammy and shivery at the thought of running into some awful indecent unpleasantness." Page 51.

Reading Hints:
Nabokov is multilingual, and English is not his first language, even though he writes it beautifully and poetically. Do not worry about any foreign phrases in the text. They are usually unimportant or are translated into English directly afterward. They are mostly there to establish Humbert Humbert as a sophisticated European gentleman.

Others by Nabokov: *Pale Fire* (novel), *Despair!* (novel), and *Laughter in the Dark* (novel).

Movies: *Lolita* (1962). Stanley Kubrick, director. Starring James Mason, Shelley Winters, Peter Sellers, and Sue Lyon.

Lolita (1998). Adrian Lyne, director. Starring Jeremy Irons, Melanie Griffith, and Dominique Swain.

Reading Icons:

Title: *Macbeth*
Author: William Shakespeare
Genre: Play Script **Number of Pages:** 30 **Date:** c. 1606
Level of Challenge: 5
Synopsis:
Is noble Macbeth's finer nature subverted by the prophecies of the three witches, or is he led to kill the good King Duncan by his own evil pride and envy? How much does Lady Macbeth have to do with the killing of the king? Can Macduff ever avenge his wife and children, and help England

heal from the wounds inflicted by civil war and social disruption? Macbeth is real history made into a thrilling story of violence and intrigue.

Quotations:

"Oftentimes, to win us to our harm./The instruments of Darkness tell us truths,/Win us with honest trifles, to betray's/In deepest consequence." Page 1222.

"Double, double, toil and trouble;/Fire burn, and cauldron bubble." Page 1237.

"I think our country sinks beneath the yoke;/It weeps, it bleeds, and each new day a gash/Is added to her wounds." Page 1241.

"Lay on, Macduff,/and damn'd be him that first cries 'Hold, enough!'" Page 1249.

Reading Hints:

Shakespeare borrowed many of his stories from other writers and from popular histories of his time. Comparison of the historical figures with the Shakespearian characters often shows how astute Shakespeare was in imagining motivations and events. Readers may want to compare Shakespeare's character Macbeth with the Scottish king of the historical accounts, just to see how much fact and how much fiction there is in Shakespeare's "history" plays.

Others by Shakespeare: *Othello* (play), *Hamlet* (play), and *The Taming of the Shrew* (play).

Movies: *Macbeth* (1948). Orson Welles, director. Starring Orson Welles, Jeannette Nolan, and Roddy McDowall.

Macbeth (1971). Roman Polanski, director. Jon Finch, Nicholas Selby, and Francesca Annis.

Reading Icons:

Title: *Madeline*

Author: Ludwig Bemelmans

Genre: Children's Book **Number of Pages:** 54 **Date:** 1939

Level of Challenge: 1 (Reading Ages 3–8)

Synopsis:

Madeline is a very special little girl, the smallest and bravest of twelve living in a house in Paris watched over by caring nuns. The twelve little girls did everything together, until one night Madeline had to go to the hospital to have her appendix removed. Madeline does so well with her operation soon all the little girls want to have their appendices removed too!

Quotations:
"In an old house in Paris/that was covered in vines/lived twelve little girls in two straight lines." Pages 1–2.

"Madeline woke up two hours/later, in a room with flowers." Page 23.

"And all the little girls cried, 'Boohoo,/we want to have our appendix out, too!'" Page 52.

Reading Hints:
Many of life's events are hard for children, and even adults, to understand fully: death, earthquakes, illness, and divorce are all puzzling. Bemelmans has the gift of finding so much joy in life that even the bad things are put into context. Readers will want to take time to enjoy the fine art illustrations of the Eiffel Tower, the Paris Opera, Notre Dame, and the Louvre.

Others by Bemelmans: *Madeline's Rescue* (children's book), *Madeline and the Bad Hat* (children's book), and *Madeline and the Gypsies* (children's book).
Movie: *Madeline* (1998). Daisy von Scherler Mayer, director. Starring Hatty Jones, Nigel Hawthorne, and Frances McDormand.

Reading Icons:

Title: *Making Friends with Frankenstein: A Book of Monstrous Poems and Pictures.*
Author: Colin McNaughton
Genre: Children's Book **Number of Pages:** 90 **Date:** 1994
Level of Challenge: 1 (Reading Ages 4–8)
Synopsis:
This is a very funny book of "gross-out" poetry for youngsters that encourages them to enjoy word play, puns, rhyme, clichés, allusions, and even kid insults. Along the way, McNaughton also suggests a number of interesting ideas about the nature of shadows and boogie-men; the importance of good manners, even in a headless man; and how to welcome an alien visitor.

Quotations:
"Cockroach sandwich/for my lunch,/Hate the taste/But love the crunch!" Page 9.

"Down in the garbage dump,/Living on the heap./Better than a pent-house—/dirt cheap!" Page 19.

"Fruit bats in the attic;/Armadillos in the hall./Piranhas in the bathtub;/Iguanas up the wall." Page 44.

"When the alien visitor/Visits our school,/Please be polite to him,/Don't play the fool." Page 62.

Reading Hints:
Adult readers may find some of the language in *Making Friends* rather juvenile, and that is, in fact, the point of many of the poems. Kid insults like "snot-rag," "pizzaface," and "stinkpot," send children into fits of childish laughter, which only the most strait-laced adult would not find infectious. This book may even take readers back to a time when bodily functions were matters of considerable humor. Relax and enjoy.
Others by McNaughton: *Wish You Were Here and I Wasn't: A Book of Poems and Pictures for Globe-Trotters* (children's book), *Here Come the Aliens!* (children's book), and *Yum!* (children's book).

Reading Icons:

Title: *The Merchant of Venice*
Author: William Shakespeare
Genre: Play Script **Number of Pages:** 31 **Date:** c. 1594
Level of Challenge: 5
Synopsis:
Characters in *The Merchant of Venice* divide their time between the masculine, thriving, mercantile seaport of Venice and Belmont, a fairyland world of love and feminine caprice. Friendships are tested, values are weighed, and loyalties are tried as Bassanio woos the fair Portia and Antonio goes to court to contest Shylock's "merry bond."
Quotations:
"But love is blind, and lovers cannot see/The pretty follies that themselves commit." Page 271.
"Sweet Bassanio, my ships have all miscarried, my creditors grow cruel, my estate is very low, my bond to the Jew is forfeit; and since in paying it, it is impossible I should live, all debts are clear'd between you and I." Page 279.
"The quality of mercy is not strain'd./It droppeth as the gentle rain from heaven/Upon the place beneath. It is twice blest;/It blesseth him that gives and him that takes." Page 284.
"How far that little candle throws his beams!/So shines a good deed in a naughty world." Page 288.
Reading Hints:
Shakespeare was not a difficult playwright in his own times. All of London came to see his plays and enjoyed them. Modern readers may need a little help with his four-hundred-year-old language, though, so a good edition of

the play, with lots of notes and annotations and helpful remarks in the margins, is a must. Bevington's *The Complete Works of Shakespeare* is excellent, as are the individual Folger editions of the plays. Readers may want to look at several complete editions of the play and pick the one that they find easiest to read.

Others by Shakespeare: *Othello* (play), *Hamlet* (play), and *The Taming of the Shrew* (play).

Movie: *The Merchant of Venice* (1973). John Sichel, director. Starring Laurence Olivier, Joan Plowright, and Jeremy Brett.

Reading Icons:

Title: *Midnight Cowboy*
Author: James Leo Herlihy
Genre: Novel **Number of Pages:** 253 **Date:** 1965
Level of Challenge: 3
Synopsis:
Joe Buck, an innocent twenty-seven-year-old, small-town boy, has a plan. He is going to New York City to take the needy women there by storm with his newly burnished "cowboy" image and his one undeniable talent. But being a male hustler in the big city is not that simple, as petty criminal Ratso Rizzo quickly proves to him. This very funny novel of dashed expectations is also a moving story of how desperately humans, even the most unlikely ones, need each other.

Quotations:
"In his new boots, Joe Buck was six-foot-one and life was different. . . . A kind of power he never even knew was there had been released in his pelvis and he was able to feel the world through it. Brand-new muscles came into play in his buttocks and in his legs, and he was aware of a totally new attitude toward the sidewalk." Page 13.

"Nowadays he had, in the person of Ratso Rizzo, someone who needed his presence in an urgent, almost frantic way that was a balm to something in him that had long been exposed and enflamed and itching to be soothed." Page 165.

"I happen to be passionate on the subject, and of course we live in an age in which all passion is suspect. All the old values have these ugly little clinical names now: Loyalty is fixation, duty is guilt, and all love is some sort of a complex!" Page 217.

Reading Hints:
Readers are no doubt aware of the "American Dream," in which a hard-working person works himself up from obscurity into a position of power and riches. Joe Buck tries to realize this dream in his own eccentric way, and by doing so asks us to evaluate seriously the dream itself. Are fame and fortune all that satisfying? Are there higher values to pursue? How important are love, companionship, and kindness in the greater scheme of things?
Others by Herlihy: *The Sleep of Baby Filbertson and Other Stories* (short stories), *All Fall Down* (novel), and *The Season of the Witch* (novel).
Movie: *Midnight Cowboy* (1969). John Schlesinger, director. Starring Dustin Hoffman, Sylvia Miles, and Jon Voight.

Reading Icons:

Title: *The Midwich Cuckoos*
Author: John Wyndham
Genre: Science Fiction Novel **Number of Pages:** 247 **Date:** 1957
Level of Challenge: 2
Synopsis:
There have been some very peculiar occurrences in the sleepy English town of Midwich. Something has landed; people and animals have been oddly, but not permanently, incapacitated; and genius children soon appear to perplex the unsuspecting residents further. What is going on, what does it mean, and how, or should, it be stopped?
Quotations:
"Do you really think one is justified in airily assuming that such a peculiar incident can just happen and then cease to happen and have no effect?" Page 55.
"The disinclination of the Children (now beginning to acquire an implied capital C, to distinguish them from other children) to be removed from the immediate neighborhood was generally accepted as just another inconvenience added to the inconveniences inevitable with babies, anyway." Page 131.
"Knowledge is simply a kind of fuel; it needs the motor of understanding to convert it into power." Page 203.
Reading Hints:
Good science fiction often asks the interesting question: "What if?" If the reader can suspend his disbelief long enough to accept the premise of the

story, no matter how far-fetched, then the rest of the action is usually quite realistic, showing how ordinary folks might act in extraordinary circumstances.

Others by Wyndham: *The Day of the Triffids* (novel), *Out of the Deeps* (novel), and *Re-Birth* (novel).

Movie: *Village of the Damned* (1960). Wolf Rilla, director. Starring George Sanders, Barbara Shelley, and Michael Gwynn.

Reading Icons:

Title: *Money: A Suicide Note*
Author: Martin Amis
Genre: Novel **Number of Pages:** 363 **Date:** 1984
Level of Challenge: 3
Synopsis:
John Self is a thirty-five-year-old British director of edgy commercials. Well heeled and well connected, he is about to make his first feature film, alternately titled *Good Money/Bad Money,* in "Sin City," New York. *Money* is a scathingly funny send-up of the 1980s, an expose of the *nouveau riche,* their excesses and their complete cluelessness.

Quotations:
"As a rule, I hate people who are the beneficiaries of a university education. . . . And you hate me, don't you. Yes you do. Because I'm the new kind, the kind who has money but can never use it for anything but ugliness." Page 59.

"Always endeavour, Slick, to keep a fix on the addiction industries: you can't lose. The addicts can't win. Dope, liquour, gambling, anything video— these have to be the deep-money veins." Page 91.

"Towards the end of a novel you get a floppy feeling. It may just be tiredness at turning the pages. People read so fast—to get to the end, to be shut of you. I see their problem. For how long do you immerse yourselves in other lives? Five minutes, but not five hours. It's a real effort." Page 331.

Reading Hints:
Martin Amis is one of the great prose stylists of our time. He is particularly good with figurative language and word play. For example: puns ("Date-raped, huh. What kind of deal is that? What, sort of with bananas and stuff?"), metaphor ("My head is a city, and various pains have now taken up residence in various parts of my face"), and personification ("The skies are

so ashamed. The trees in the squares hang their heads"). Writers who want to improve their own personal styles may want to study Amis's techniques. **Others by Amis:** *London Fields* (novel), *Visiting Mrs. Nabokov* (essays), and *The Information* (novel).

Reading Icons:

Title: *The Murder of Roger Ackroyd*
Author: Agatha Christie
Genre: Mystery Novel **Number of Pages:** 255 **Date:** 1926
Level of Challenge: 2
Synopsis:
Agatha Christie is famous for her eccentric little Belgian detective Hercule Poirot. In this mystery novel, Poirot, who has gone into retirement in the sleepy English village of King's Abbot, is drawn into one of the most complex mysteries of his career. Readers who think that mysteries are too simple and that "the butler did it" will find their minds and intuitions fully taxed by this unusual tale.
Quotations:
"The essence of a detective story . . . is to have a rare poison—if possible something from South America, that nobody has ever heard of—something that one obscure tribe of savages use to poison their arrows with. Death is instantaneous, and Western Science is powerless to detect it." Page 23.
"'It is completely unimportant' said Poirot. 'That is why it is so interesting,' he added softly." Page 84.
"The truth, however ugly in itself, is always curious and beautiful to the seeker after it." Page 135.
"After all, many crimes have been committed for the sake of less than five hundred pounds. It all depends on what sum is sufficient to break a man. A question of the relativity, is it not so?" Page 159.
Reading Hints:
Mystery novels are highly plot driven. The reader must be at constant attention, searching for clues, testing hypothesis, letting her intuition play, in order to beat the detective to the solution, or at least to understand the solution when it is exposed at the end of the book.
Others by Christie: *Murder on the Orient Express* (Hercule Poirot mystery novel), *A Pocket Full of Rye* (Jane Marple mystery novel), and *Evil under the Sun* (Hercule Poirot mystery novel).

Movie: Although there is no movie of *The Murder of Roger Ackroyd* (yet), most of the other Poirot stories are available on DVD in the fine TV series *Agatha Christie's Poirot*.

Reading Icons:

Title: *Murphy's Law*
Author: Rhys Bowen
Genre: Mystery Novel **Number of Pages:** 226 **Date:** 2001
Level of Challenge: 2
Synopsis:
Molly Murphy, the plucky Irish "murderess" and amateur sleuth, arrives at Ellis Island in turn-of-the-century New York hoping to put her past behind her, only to find herself embroiled in a complicated, political murder plot. Fans of Bowen's Constable Evans mysteries will enjoy her clever and charming new protagonist.
Quotations:
"I loved those lessons. There never could be enough books in the world for me. I devoured them all, geography and history and even Shakespeare and Latin." Page 29.
"How could I possibly prove he was innocent? The answer came immediately: by finding the one who is guilty." Page 109.
"It didn't take long to realize one thing. New York was not an American city. It was a collection of small Italian, Jewish, German and God knows what else villages, all slapped down next to each other." Page 116.
"Our clothing must surely have been designed by men to make sure we were hindered in matters of self-defence." Page 141.
Reading Hints:
It is easy to underestimate the value of an easy-to-read and entertaining novel like Bowen's *Murphy's Law*. But in it readers are lead effortlessly to a greater understanding of the reasons for Irish immigration to America at the turn of the century, the complicated intake processes of Ellis Island, and the nationality-driven ward politics of early New York City.
Others by Bowen: *Evanly Choirs* (mystery novel), *Evan Can Wait* (mystery novel), and *Death of Riley* (mystery novel).

Reading Icons:

Title: *The Name of the Rose*
Author: Umberto Eco
Genre: Gothic Novel **Number of Pages:** 611 **Date:** 1980
Level of Challenge: 4
Synopsis:
An English monk, Brother William of Baskerville, has been dispatched to a fourteenth-century Italian abbey where he finds a series of curious and inexplicable murders. His job is to find the murderer and unravel the secrets of the enormous Aedificium (library). The spiritual conundrums are as complex as the crimes.
Quotations:
"Adelmo of Otranto, a monk still young though already famous as a master illuminator, who had been decorating the manuscripts of the library with the most beautiful images, had been found one morning by a goatherd at the bottom of the cliff below the Aedificium." Page 29.
"And finally as the great Roger Bacon warned, the secrets of science must not always pass into the hands of all, for some could use them to evil ends. Often the learned man must make seem magic certain books that are not magic, but simply good science, in order to protect them from indiscreet eyes." Page 98.
"The theological virtues are three, and three are the holy languages, the parts of the soul, the classes of intellectual creatures, angels, men and devils; There are three kinds of sound—vox, flatus, pulsus—and three epochs of human history, before, during, and after the law." Page 540.
Reading Hints:
The Name of the Rose has a map of the abbey in the front matter; the buildings play an important part in the plot. Readers will find the action easier to follow if they refer to that map carefully throughout their reading of the novel.
Others by Eco: *Foucault's Pendulum* (novel), *Baudolino* (novel), and *The Bomb and the General* (children's book).
Movie: *The Name of the Rose* (1986). Jean-Jaques Annaud, director. Starring Sean Connery, F. Murray Abraham, and Christian Slater.

Reading Icons:

Title: *Night Shift*
Author: Stephen King
Genre: Short Stories **Number of Pages:** 326 **Date:** 1979

Level of Challenge: 2
Synopsis:
Stephen King is an acknowledged master of horror fiction and as he puts it: "The tale of monstrosity and terror is a basket loosely packed with phobias; when the writer passes by, you take one of his imaginary horrors out of the basket and put one of your real ones in—at least for a time." This short story collection has a basket of horrors including: vampires, evil children, stalkers, giant rats, serial murderers, and space vermin—something to scare everyone.
Quotations:
"I felt comfortable as only one can on such a night, when all is miserable outside and all is warmth and comfort inside; but a moment later Cal appeared at the door, looking excited and bit nervous." Page 7.
"Two young girls and some old Salvation Army wino had disappeared in the town during the last three weeks or so—all after dark." Page 115.
"From all around the children were coming. Some of them were laughing gaily. They held knives, hatchets, pipes, rocks, hammers. One girl, maybe eight, with beautiful long blond hair, held a jackhandle." Page 269.
"But now all the dirt and all the crap was gone. The ocean had eaten it, all of it, as casually as you might eat a handful of Cracker Jacks. There were no people to come back and dirty it again. Just us, and we weren't enough to make much mess." Page 53.
Reading Hints:
Horror fiction and roller coasters share the same essential appeal: humans love to be frightened—safely. King has a special gift for making familiar things terrifying. He sees as much potential for evil and mayhem in a lawn-mower or a bouquet of flowers as he does in mutant rodents or worldwide flu epidemics. Readers who are also writers may want to examine how he manages to find the grotesque in something as simple as trying to quit smoking.
Others by King: *Carrie* (novel), *Christine* (novel), and *Cujo* (novel).
Movies: *Salem's Lot* (1979). Tobe Hooper, director. Starring James Mason, David Soul, and Marie Windsor.
Children of the Corn (1984). Fritz Kiersch, director. Starring Peter Horton, Linda Hamilton, and Courtney Gains.

Reading Icons:

: *Nocturne*
   or: Adam Rapp

Genre: Play Script **Number of Pages:** 81 **Date:** 2001
Level of Challenge: 4
Synopsis:
A thirty-two year old man, a pianist-turned-author, looks back on his life after a fatal car accident in which he accidentally killed his beloved sister. The effects on his mother, father, and himself are as unexpected as they are inevitable.
Quotations:
"Fifteen years ago I killed my sister. There. I said it." Page 7.
"He would stare at the typewriter as though it was some sort of singing tropical fish. He would wait for it to break into song for roughly two years." Page 43.
"I've lost my name. I've turned into that anonymous, boyish pronoun used by policemen and coaches: 'Son.'" Page 34.
Reading Hints:
Rapp uses musical terms with great grace and precision. You might want to look up words like "sonata," "fugue," and "nocturne" to enjoy fully his language and his plotting. From his choice of words to the ordering of his scenes and acts, Rapp's play is constructed with the care and finesse of a fine musical composition.
Others by Rapp: *Missing the Piano* (novel), *The Buffalo Tree* (novel), and *The Copper Elephant* (novel).

Reading Icons:

Title: *Oranges Are Not the Only Fruit*
Author: Jeanette Winterson
Genre: Novel **Number of Pages:** 176 **Date:** 1985
Level of Challenge: 3
Synopsis:
Jeanette Winterson's autobiographical first novel explores the experiences of a young woman, groomed to be an evangelical preacher, whose life takes an unexpected turn as she comes to terms with her own budding sexuality. This unusual coming-of-age story, organized around the books of the Bible, is as universal as it is eccentric, as hilarious as it is serious.
Quotations:
"Elsie came every day, and told me jokes to make me smile and stories to make me feel better. She said stories helped you to understand the world." Page 29.

"The Heathen were a daily household preoccupation. My mother found them everywhere, particularly Next Door. They tormented her as only the godless can, but she had her methods." Page 53.

"So there I was, my success in the pulpit being the reason for my downfall. The devil had attacked me at my weakest point: my inability to realize the limitations of my sex." Page 134.

"I can't settle, I want someone who is fierce and will love me until death and know that love is as strong as death, and be on my side for ever and ever. I want someone who will destroy and be destroyed by me." Page 170.

Reading Hints:
There are a number of parables, mythic stories, and fairy tales in this novel. At first they might seem to be extraneous, but on closer examination they always relate quite clearly to the journey of the heroine. Readers will want to see how many of the correlations they can ferret out.

Others by Winterson: *Written on the Body* (novel), *The Passion* (novel), and *The World and Other Places* (short stories).

Movie: *Oranges Are Not the Only Fruit* (1989). Beeban Kidron, director. Starring Geraldine McEwan, Charlotte Coleman, and Kenneth Cranham.

Reading Icons:

Title: *Othello*
Author: William Shakespeare
Genre: Play Script **Number of Pages:** 43 **Date:** c. 1603
Level of Challenge: 5
Synopsis:
Othello is the most domestic of Shakespeare's great tragedies. Othello, a noble Moorish general, is played upon by his evil subordinate Iago to doubt the fidelity of his beautiful, fair wife Desdemona. Powerful issues of envy, race, class, and gender make *Othello* just as timely today as it was in seventeenth-century England.

Quotations:
"She love'd me for the dangers I had pass'd,/And I lov'd her that she did pity them./That is the only witchcraft I have us'd." Page 1131.

"Look to her, Moor, if thou hast eyes to see./She has deceiv'd her father, and may thee." Page 1133.

"I think my wife be honest and think she is not;/I think that thou art just and think thou art not./I'll have some proof." Page 1148.

"Then must you speak/Of one that lov'd not wisely but too well." Page 1167.

Reading Hints:

Shakespeare's plays were meant to be performed, and each version of the play, on stage or screen, represents one director's interpretation of the text. Readers need to be their own directors and will want to imagine an ideal cast, design perfect sets and costumes, and supply all of the needed gestures and actions to make Shakespeare's words clear to themselves and others. One of the great joys of theater-going is comparing different productions of Shakespeare's masterpieces with each other and with one's own ideas about the plays.

Others by Shakespeare: *Merchant of Venice* (play), *Hamlet* (play), and *The Taming of the Shrew* (play).

Movies: *Othello* (1952). Orson Welles, director. Starring Orson Welles, Micheál MacLiammóir, and Suzanne Cloutier.

Othello (1965). Stuart Burge, director. Starring Laurence Olivier, Frank Finlay, and Maggie Smith.

Othello (1995). Oliver Parker, director. Starring Laurence Fishburne, Irene Jacob, and Kenneth Branagh.

Reading Icons:

Title: *The Phantom of the Opera*
Author: Gaston Leroux
Genre: Gothic Novel **Number of Pages:** 264 **Date:** 1911
Level of Challenge: 4
Synopsis:

The Phantom of the Opera is part gothic novel, part mystery, and part romance. There is great confusion about the real identity of the whimsical and dangerous opera ghost who is plaguing the magnificent nineteenth-century Opera House in Paris; there is no question, however, that he has a special power over Christine Daae and unfettered access to this labyrinthine temple to music.

Quotations:

"None will ever be a true Parisian who has not learned to wear a mask of gaiety over his sorrows and one of sadness, boredom, or indifference over his inward joy. . . . In Paris, our lives are one masked ball." Page 28.

"I saw a terrible death's head, which darted a look at me from a pair of scorching eyes. I felt as if I were face to face with Satan; and, in the presence of this unearthly apparition, my heart gave way, my courage failed me." Page 63.

"Raoul's first thought, after Christine Daae's fantastic disappearance, was to accuse Erik. He no longer doubted the almost supernatural powers of the Angel of Music, in this domain of the Opera in which he had set up his empire." Page 150.

Reading Hints:

Sometimes there is a remarkable connection between a work of literature and a work of architecture. The reader's enjoyment of this book will be much enhanced by finding out something about the Opera House in Paris—or better yet, visiting it in person.

Others by Leroux: *The Mystery of the Yellow Room* (mystery novel) and *The Double Life of Theophraste Longuet* (mystery novel).

Movies: *The Phantom of the Opera* (1925). Rupert Julian, director. Starring Lon Chaney and Mary Philbin.

The Phantom of the Opera (1943). Arthur Lubin, director. Starring Claude Rains, Nelson Eddy, and Hume Cronyn.

Reading Icons:

Title: *The Picture of Dorian Gray*
Author: Oscar Wilde
Genre: Gothic Novel **Number of Pages:** 300 **Date:** 1891
Level of Challenge: 4
Synopsis:

The eternally young and beautiful Dorian Gray is harboring a dark secret. Torn between artist Basil Hallward's love of him and his fascination with the decadent aesthete Lord Henry, Dorian Gray lives a life of excruciating luxury and pain, affecting all the men and women who cross his path.

Quotations:

"Dorian Gray had been poisoned by a book. There were moments when he looked on evil simply as a mode through which he could realize his conception of the beautiful." Page 158.

"One could never pay too high a price for any sensation." Page 72.

"There were opium dens where one could buy oblivion, dens of horror where the memory of old sins could be destroyed by the madness of sins that were new." Page 196.

"Is insincerity such a terrible thing? I think not. It is merely a method by which we can multiply our personalities." Page 154.

Reading Hints:
While *The Picture of Dorian Gray* is an exciting gothic novel with an intricate plot, it is also a book that explores the moral implications of a philosophy that judges everything by aesthetic criteria: is it beautiful, does it excite, is it new and unusual? Readers might want to think about their own ideas about the relationship between beauty and goodness.
Others by Wilde: *Lady Windermere's Fan* (play), "The Ballad of Reading Gaol" (poem), and "Lord Arthur Savile's Crime" (short story).
Movie: *The Picture of Dorian Gray* (1945). Albert Lewin, director. Starring Hurd Hatfield, Donna Reed, Peter Lawford, and Angela Lansbury.

Reading Icons:

Title: *The Pillars of the Earth*
Author: Ken Follett
Genre: Historical Novel **Number of Pages:** 973 **Date:** 1989
Level of Challenge: 3
Synopsis:
The Pillars of the Earth will appeal to readers interested in everyday life in the Middle Ages, English church politics, and most of all, the building of the great gothic cathedrals by master builders, who were inventing the laws of architecture as they went along. Historical accuracy, rich characterization, and a pleasing writing style made this novel a national bestseller.
Quotations:
"The new leaves were coming out. Tom had always been taught to decorate the cushion capitals on top of the piers with scrolls or zigzags, but now it occurred to him that decorations in the shape of leaves would look rather striking." Page 397.
"Aliena felt humiliated, and Richard had the grace to look a little shamefaced. The two men had been negotiating over her like horse dealers. She got to her feet, and without another word she left the house." Page 617.
"All right, he admitted, my motives are tainted and my ability is in doubt. Perhaps I should refuse to stand. At least I could be sure to avoid the sin of pride. But what was it that Cuthbert had said? 'A man may just as easily frustrate the will of God through excessive humility.'" Page 137.
Reading Hints:
Readers can learn as much good history from a well-researched historical novel as from a history book. Don't forget that much of this novel relies on

real historical events, real historical personages, and the most reliable information available to scholars about the life of the times.

Others by Follett: *Eye of the Needle* (novel), *Jackdaws* (novel), and *Night over Water* (novel).

Reading Icons:

Title: *Pnin*
Author: Vladimir Nabokov
Genre: Novel **Number of Pages:** 191 **Date:** 1953
Level of Challenge: 4
Synopsis:
A charming, intrusive, and chatty narrator tells the genteel story of Professor Timofey Pnin, an emigre "Russian-intelligentski" who comes to teach at an American college in the mid-twentieth century. Pnin is a prototypical absent-minded professor, who mangles the English language, is obsessed with the time line of *Anna Karenina,* and finds a touching pleasure in the smallest good fortune. In this simple narrative guise, a mystery is worked out and a good deal of philosophy is quietly expressed.

Quotations:
"Some people—and I am one of them—hate happy ends. We feel cheated. Harm is the norm. Doom should not jam. The avalanche stopping in its tracks a few feet above the cowering village behaves not only unnaturally but unethically." Page 26.

"Next, they switched to the usual shop talk of European teachers abroad, sighing and shaking heads over the 'typical American college student' who does not know geography, is immune to noise, and thinks education is but a means to get eventually a remunerative job." Pages 125–26.

"Our friend employs a nomenclature all his own. His verbal vagaries add a new thrill to life. His mispronunciations are mythopeic. His slips of the tongue are oracular. He calls my wife John." Page 165.

"Genius is non-conformity." Page 89.

Reading Hints:
Readers might enjoy thinking about teachers and professors whom they have known personally and comparing them to Professor Pnin. Novels can make excellent writing prompts for readers who want to improve their observation, language, and narrative skills. Beloved, cruel, peculiar, or irritating teachers make excellent subjects for small or extended portraits.

Others by Nabokov: *Lolita* (novel), *Pale Fire* (novel), and *Tyrants Destroyed and Other Stories* (short stories).

Reading Icons:

Title: *Postmodern Pooh*
Author: Frederick Crews
Genre: Parody **Number of Pages:** 175 **Date:** 2001
Level of Challenge: 4
Synopsis:
Frederick Crews, professor of English at the University of California at Berkeley, has written a hilarious parody of freshman literary casebooks. Eleven separate chapters lampoon every major modern critical school, using A. A. Milne's *Winnie the Pooh* as their subject. No critical approach to literature is left unmolested.
Quotations:
"And what can I say, except get a life, to people who still yearn to have their 'values' validated by books—the killer app of the 1400s." Page 136.
"Children are, after all, not a breed apart but merely very short people whose self-control and range of allusions still want improving." Page 159.
"And for that matter, literature itself exists only insofar as we critics constitute it as such, cordoning off certain clumps of squiggles as aesthetic objects." Page 169.
Reading Hints:
Although anyone can enjoy this book, it is a lot more fun for readers who have already read *Winnie the Pooh*. It is even more fun for readers who know a little something about feminist, marxist, and queer studies schools of criticism.
Another by Crews: *The Pooh Perplex* (parody).

Reading Icons:

Title: *Prey*
Author: Michael Crichton
Genre: Science Fiction **Number of Pages:** 364 **Date:** 2002
Level of Challenge: 2
Synopsis:
Prey is a suspenseful novel about what could happen in the future at the meeting points of three fledgling technologies: nanotechnology, biotechnology,

and computer technology. What happens when scientists play God, experiments take on lives of their own, and people have to live with the horror of unintended consequences?

Quotations:

"There's one problem with all psychological knowledge—nobody can apply it to themselves. People can be incredibly astute about the shortcomings of their friends, spouses, children. But they have no insight into themselves at all." Page 77.

"The Pentagon wanted a camera that couldn't be shot down. They imagined something very small, maybe the size of a dragonfly—a target too small to hit." Page 124.

"You've got a breakaway robotic nanoswarm. That some idiot made self-powered and self-sustaining." Page 150.

"Human beings tended to believe that without central command, chaos would overwhelm the organization and nothing significant could be accomplished. " Page 274.

Reading Hints:

Classic science fiction by authors like Jules Verne, Mary Shelley, and H. G. Wells were not really that interested in science. For example, in the novel *Frankenstein,* almost no time is spent describing the actual creation of the monster. Modern readers, however, demand extremely exact and up-to-date information in their science fiction, so newer novels tend to be, among other things, remarkably and painlessly educational.

Others by Crichton: *The Andromeda Strain* (science fiction), *Jurassic Park* (science fiction), and *The Terminal Man* (science fiction).

Reading Icons:

Title: *Rebecca*
Author: Daphne DuMaurier
Genre: Romance Novel **Number of Pages:** 380 **Date:** 1938
Level of Challenge: 2
Synopsis:

This is the story of Rebecca, the first Mrs. de Winter, mysteriously drowned, as told by the second Mrs. de Winter, who tries timidly but steadfastly to live up to the exalted image of her much-admired predecessor. Does Maxim de Winter, the husband, or Mrs. Danvers, the loyal waiting maid, know the secret at the center of the Manderley mansion, and will the
ler ever find out?

Quotations:
"It's Max de Winter, " she said, "the man who owns Manderley. You've heard of it, of course. He looks ill, doesn't he? They say he can't get over his wife's death." Page 11.

"Never mind, I'll take you to Venice for our honeymoon and we'll hold hands in the gondola. But we won't stay too long because I want to show you Manderley." Page 53.

"Do you think the dead come back and watch the living? Sometimes I wonder if she [Rebecca] comes back here to Manderley and watches you and Mr. de Winter together." Page 172.

Reading Hints:
Mysteries in novels, and in real life, depend very often on everyone's being dedicated to keeping certain information secret. Often each person has only one piece of the puzzle, and it isn't until they all cooperate that the mystery is solved. Readers who are very clever can sometimes put the puzzle together before the characters discover the complete truth.

Others by DuMaurier: *Jamaica Inn* (novel), *The Scapegoat* (novel), and *My Cousin Rachel* (novel).

Movie: *Rebecca* (1940). Alfred Hitchcock, director. Starring Laurence Olivier, Joan Fontaine, and George Sanders.

Reading Icons:

Title: *A River Sutra*
Author: Gita Mehta
Genre: Novel **Number of Pages:** 291 **Date:** 1993
Level of Challenge: 4
Synopsis:
The narrator has left an active life in India's great cities to take up a vacant post at a government rest house situated on the Narmada River, one of India's holiest pilgrimage sites. In this jungle retreat, full of teak and banyans, he seeks personal enlightenment with the help of his clerk, his friend the mullah of the village mosque, and the passing pilgrims who share his quest and sometimes his otherwise quiet life. This sutra is held together by the waters of the great Narmada River and all who seek enlightenment there.

Quotations:
"Many are like myself, quite elderly persons who have completed the first stages of life prescribed by our Hindu scriptures—the infant, the student,

the householder—and who have now entered the stage of the vanaprasthi, to seek personal enlightenment." Page 7.

"At the age of twenty-six I had already become fatigued by the world, knowing that even at the moment of gratification, the seed of new desire was being sown." Page 29.

"I hope you are not contracting the fatal Indian disease of making everything holy, my friend. The Narmada is already too holy by half. Do you know how many sacred spots there are supposed to be on her banks? Four hundred billion." Page 151.

Reading Hints:

There are many traditions of story-telling in which a series of disparate but interconnected stories are held together by a single narrator or idea. *The Canterbury Tales, The Arabian Nights,* and *The Decameron* all share with *A River Sutra* this common literary device. Readers will enjoy seeing how cleverly Mehta joins one story seamlessly to the next and how all the stories lead to the narrator's and the readers' eventual enlightenment.

Others by Mehta: *Karma Cola* (novel) and *Raj* (novel).

Reading Icons:

Title: *The Robber Bride*
Author: Margaret Atwood
Genre: Novel **Number of Pages:** 466 **Date:** 1993
Level of Challenge: 4
Synopsis:

Zenia is Margaret Atwood's Iago, a woman with no redeeming virtues, no compensatory motivations, and no scruples. Her devastating effect on the lives of military historian Tony, New Age yoga teacher Charis, and canny businesswoman Roz forms the basis of a wildly funny, yet persistently dark, novel in which all the major players are women.

Quotations:

"Male historians think she's invading their territory, and should leave their spears, arrows, catapults, lances, swords, guns, planes and bombs alone. They think she should be writing social history, such as who ate what when, or Life in the Feudal Family. Female historians, of whom there are not many, think the same thing but for different reasons." Page 21.

"Shanita has never had a dose of Zenia. She won't realize, she can't understand Zenia can't be meditated out of existence. If she could be, Charis would have done it long ago." Page 68.

"Roz's money is plentiful, but it needs to be aged, like good wine or cheese. It's too brash, too shiny, too exclamatory. It's too brazen." Page 341.
"Maybe that was Zenia's trick. Maybe she presented herself as vacancy, as starvation, as an empty beggar's bowl." Page 368.

Reading Hints:
If Zenia is evil incarnate, what might the other women in this rich, multi-layered novel represent? When an author presents the reader with three very different characters, all being preyed upon by the same person, it is useful to ask what about each of them makes her a probable victim.

Others by Atwood: *The Handmaid's Tale* (science fiction), *Cat's Eye* (novel), and *Wilderness Tips* (short stories).

Reading Icons:

Title: *San Francisco Stories*
Editor: John Miller
Genre: Various **Number of Pages:** 299 **Date:** 1990
Level of Challenge: 3
Synopsis:
John Miller has collected some of the finest writing ever done about the city of San Francisco. In this volume, readers will find Amy Tan telling about growing up in America's largest Chinatown; Randy Shilts explaining the assassination of San Francisco mayor Moscone, and gay supervisor Harvey Milk; Mark Twain expounding on the "glories" of the famous Cliff House before dawn; and Lewis H. Lapham admitting why he finally left California for the East Coast.

Quotations:
"This collection turns the postcard of San Francisco over and allows us to read the messages on the back. That is, we've decided to pass by travel-brochure description in favor of writing that shows the secret city." Page ix (John Miller).
"One after another, electric signs with neon martini glasses lit up on them, the San Francisco symbol of 'bar'—thousands of neon-magenta martini glasses bouncing and streaming down the hill." Page 3 (Tom Wolfe).
"We lived in San Francisco's Chinatown. Like most of the other Chinese children who played in the back alleys of restaurants and curio shops, I didn't think we were poor." Page 110 (Amy Tan).
"Show me a group of at least reasonably successful writers, actors, filmmak-ers, fine artists, and dancers, and I'll show you a litter of weird, tortured puppies." Page 262 (Anne Lamott).

Reading Hints:
This compilation contains a wide range of genres: obscure poems, passionate essays, three-dot columns, excerpts from novels, reportage, autobiography, news dispatches, and short stories. Readers will want to see if they can discern differences between the writers of gonzo journalism, nonfiction essays, and fictional accounts.

Others by Miller: *Lust: Lascivious Love Stories and Passionate Poems* (various), *Christmas Stories: Tales of the Season* (various), and *On Suicide: Great Writers on the Ultimate Question* (various).

Reading Icons:

Title: *The Secret Agent*
Author: Joseph Conrad
Genre: Novel **Number of Pages:** 269 **Date:** 1907
Level of Challenge: 3
Synopsis:
In Victorian England, London was the target of anarchists, who were, not unlike today's terrorists, loosely organized, fervent in their beliefs, and largely ineffectual. Conrad's novel *The Secret Agent* throws an ironic light on everything from the subversives' private lives to the complicity of the government in their illegal activities. This is an excellent example of a novel, approaching its hundredth birthday, that is just as relevant and interesting today as it was on the day it was written.

Quotations:
"All these people had to be protected. Protection is the first necessity of opulence and luxury. They had to be protected; and their horses, carriages, houses, servants had to be protected." Page 51.

"A bomb outrage to have any influence on public opinion now must go beyond the intention of vengeance or terrorism. . . . Madness alone is truly terrifying, inasmuch as you cannot placate it either by threats, persuasion, or bribes." Pages 66–67.

"The way of even the most justifiable revolutions is prepared by personal impulses disguised into creeds." Page 102.

"Curiosity being one of the forms of self-revelation, a systematically incurious person remains always partly mysterious." Page 216.

Reading Hints:
Conrad got some of the ideas for this novel from an actual attempt in 1894 to blow up the Greenwich Observatory, just outside London. Readers who

are also writers might enjoy searching their local newspaper for the kernel of a good story. Many important works of literature have been written on the slender thread of a plot suggested by a newspaper or magazine article. **Others by Conrad:** *Nostromo* (novel), *Heart of Darkness* (short story), and *Typhoon* (novel).

Movies: *Sabotage* (1936). Alfred Hitchcock, director. Starring Oskar Homolka and Sylvia Sydney.

The Secret Agent (1996). Christopher Hampton, director. Starring Bob Hoskins, Patricia Arquette, and Robin Williams.

Reading Icons:

Title: *The Secret Garden*
Author: Frances Hodgson Burnett
Genre: Children's Novel **Number of Pages:** 311 **Date:** 1911
Level of Challenge: 1
Synopsis:
Mary Lennox arrived at Misselthwaite Manor orphaned and lonely, only to find her uncle's York manor a place of many wonders. There was Dickon, with his special relationship with animals and birds; there was Colin, crippled by the burden of adult sorrows; and there was, most importantly, the magical secret garden, where everyone learns the healing powers of nature, the innocence of childhood, and the importance of having and sharing secrets.

Quotations:
"When Mary Lennox was sent to Misselthwaite manor to live with her uncle everybody said she was the most disagreeable looking child ever seen. It was true, too." Page 3.

"Mother says as th' two worst things as can happen to a child is never to have his own way—or always to have it." Page 191.

"Four good things had happened to her, in fact, since she came to Misselthwaite Manor. She had felt as if she had understood a robin and that he had understood her; she had run in the wind until her blood had grown warm; she had been healthily hungry for the first time in her life; and she had found out what it was to be sorry for some one." Page 52.

Reading Hints:
While adult novels often espouse complete philosophies, children's books frequently make simple but useful moral points. Adult readers will want to

ferret out these moral principles for themselves, and also to call them to the attention of any young people to whom they are reading.

Others by Burnett: *A Little Princess* (children's novel) and *Little Lord Fauntleroy* (children's novel).

Movies: *The Secret Garden* (1949). Fred M. Wilcox, director. Starring Margaret O'Brien, Herbert Marshall, and Gladys Cooper.

The Secret Garden (1993). Agnieszka Holland, director. Starring Kate Maberly, Maggie Smith, and John Lynch.

Reading Icons:

Title: *Shane*
Author: Jack Schaefer
Genre: Western Novel **Number of Pages:** 151 **Date:** 1949
Level of Challenge: 2
Synopsis:
Shane is the classic western about the feud between open-range cattle ranchers and homesteading farmers. Shane is a cowboy who is larger than life to the young boy who narrates this tale of fierce loyalty, manly virtue, and respect for hard work.

Quotations:
"He [Shane] rode into our valley in the summer of '89. I was a kid then, barely topping the backboard of father's old chuck-wagon." Page 1.

"I like that. A man who watches what's going on around him will make his mark." Page 6.

"A gun is as good—and as bad—as the man who carries it. Remember that." Page 55.

"A man can keep his self-respect without having to cram it down another man's throat." Page 81.

Reading Hints:
The narrator of this story is a young boy, Bob, who is frankly star-struck by Shane and continually says that what is going on in the story is "beyond [his] understanding." It would be unwise, however, to take Bob at his word for this. Readers will want to notice how cleverly this young man manages to be at every single important event in the novel and how faithfully he records all of the important bits of conversation. He turns out to be quite a competent narrator despite all his manly modesty.

Others by Schaefer: *Monte Walsh* (novel), *The Collected Short Stories of Jack Schaefer* (short stories), and *First Blood* (novel).

Movie: *Shane* (1953). George Stevens, director. Starring Alan Ladd, Jack Palance, and Van Heflin.

Reading Icons:

Title: *Sheep in Wolves' Clothing*
Author: Satoshi Kitamura
Genre: Children's Book **Number of Pages:** 30 **Date:** 1995
Level of Challenge: 1 (Reading Ages 4–8)
Synopsis:
Kitamura has taken the common cliché "A Wolf in Sheep's Clothing" and completely turned it around in a witty story with extravagantly colorful and complex illustrations. Sheep drive cars, wolves knit sweaters, and kittens play rugby in this highly imaginative romp.
Quotations:
"The three sheep sat around the car. What could they do?" Page 6.
"Four wolves were playing miniature golf on the sand." Page 9.
"They seemed so kind. . . . But perhaps they weren't!" Page 11.
"Whoever heard of a sheep picking a fight with wolves?" Page 22.
Reading Hints:
Many fables and fairy tales written for children but enjoyed by adults have characters that are animals. These animals, however, usually act like humans. For example, one of the sheep in this story is "Elliot Baa, private detective." Readers may like to ponder why certain kinds of animals are chosen for certain types of roles. Personification, or giving an animal the characteristics of a human, is a common form of creative writing in adult fiction and poetry as well.
Others by Kitamura: *A Boy Wants a Dinosaur* (children's book), *What's Inside? The Alphabet Book* (children's book), *When Sheep Cannot Sleep: The Counting Book* (children's book).

Reading Icons:

Title: *Slaughterhouse Five*
Author: Kurt Vonnegut Jr.
Genre: Novel **Number of Pages:** 215 **Date:** 1968
Level of Challenge: 5

Synopsis:
Billy Pilgrim is unstuck in time, possibly resulting from his survival of the Dresden fire-bombing in World War II, a commercial airliner crash, or an alien abduction. This antiwar novel, told from the point of view of a "casualty," is improbably humorous and warmhearted.

Quotations:
"So then I understood. It was war that made her so angry. She didn't want her babies or anybody else's babies killed in wars. And she thought wars were partly encouraged by books and movies." Page 15.

"There are almost no characters in this story, and almost no dramatic confrontations, because most of the people in it are so sick and so much the listless playthings of enormous forces. One of the main effects of war, after all, is that people are discouraged from being characters." Page 164.

"All he does in his sleep is quit and surrender and apologize and ask to be left alone." Page 184.

Reading Hints:
This story is not told chronologically. It appears to jump about senselessly, but it is actually very well organized by associated thoughts. Readers will want to watch carefully to see how each section is linked through images, language, or ideas.

Others by Vonnegut Jr.: *The Sirens of Titan* (science fiction), *Cat's Cradle* (novel), and *Jailbird* (novel). Vonnegut graded his own novels and gave these As.

Movie: *Slaughterhouse Five* (1972). George Roy Hill, director. Starring Michael Sacks, Ron Leibman, and Valerie Perrine.

Reading Icons:

Title: *The Sneeches and Other Stories*
Author: Dr. Seuss
Genre: Children's Book   **Number of Pages:** 65 **Date:** 1961
Level of Challenge: 1 (Reading Ages 4–8)
Synopsis:
This is the story of the Star-Belly Sneeches and the Plain-Belly sort, and the clever Sylvester McMonkey McBean, who made lots and lots of money by taking advantage of their silly prejudices. This charming book also contains the stories "Too Many Daves," "The Zax," and "What Was I Scared Of?"

Quotations:
"Now, the Star-Belly Sneetches/Had bellies with stars./The Plain-Belly Sneetches/Had none upon thars." Page 1.
"One day, making tracks/In the prairie of Prax,/Came a North-Going Zax/And a South-Going Zax." Page 27.
"Did I ever tell you that Mrs. McCave/Had twenty-three sons and she named them all Dave?" Page 36.

Reading Hints:
Dr. Seuss was way ahead of his time in fostering harmony among people with differences. Even though his stories are full of nonsense words and silly rhymes, they almost always have a useful moral for young children. Readers will want to have lots of fun with words like "Sneeches" and "Zanzibar Buck-Buck McFate," but they will probably also want to talk with their fortunate children about the ideas in the stories as well.

Others by Seuss: *Horton Hatches the Egg* (children's book), *How the Grinch Stole Christmas!* (children's book), and *The Lorax* (children's book).

Reading Icons:

Title: *The Summer before the Dark*
Author: Doris Lessing
Genre: Novel **Number of Pages:** 247 **Date:** May 1973
Level of Challenge: 4
Synopsis:
Kate Brown, British, forty-five years old, married for a quarter of a century, is faced with her first free summer since she was a young girl. In two short months, packed with a lifetime of experiences, contemplation, anguish, and epiphanies, Kate finds herself and her place in the universe.

Quotations:
"The truth was, she was becoming more and more uncomfortably conscious not only that the things she said, and a good many of the things she thought, had been taken down off a rack and put on, but that what she really felt was something else again." Page 2.
"In a moment, they, Jeffrey and she, would be outbidding each other in that most common of middle-class verbal games: which of them had acquired more grace by being close to other people's sufferings." Page 78.
"She had lived among words, and people bred to use and be used by words." Page 244.

Reading Hints:
Post-Freud, many authors became interested in the kinds of dreams their characters might have. There is a recurring dream about a "seal" in this novel. Watch the progress of the dream and its relationship to Kate Brown's feelings and life.

Others by Lessing: *The Memoirs of a Survivor* (novel), *Mara and Dann* (science fiction), and *A Proper Marriage* (novel).

Reading Icons:

Title: *The Taming of the Shrew*
Author: William Shakespeare
Genre: Play Script **Number of Pages:** 33 **Date:** c. 1592
Level of Challenge: 5
Synopsis:
Fair Bianca will never get married if her family does not find a suitor for her older, shrewish sister Katharina. Luckily, Petruchio is in need of a dowry and a wife. This is the story of his energetic wooing of this spirited and difficult woman. Like many of Shakespeare's comedies, *Taming* has lots of reversals and surprises, and a full complement of weddings at the end.

Quotations:
"Gentlemen, importune me no farther,/for how I firmly am resolv'd you know:/That is, not to bestow my youngest daughter/ Before I have a husband for the elder." Page 197.

"Well, come, my Kate. We will unto your father's/Even in these honest mean habiliments./Our purses shall be proud, our garments poor,/for 'tis the mind that makes the body rich." Page 219.

"Katharina, I charge thee, tell these headstrong women/What duty they do owe their lords and husbands." Page 226.

Reading Hints:
Shakespeare's plays are usually classified as comedies, histories, or tragedies. Modern readers will be struck with how many tremendously funny scenes there are in the tragedies (the porter in *Macbeth*, the grave digger in *Hamlet*), and how many rather serious scenes there are in the comedies (Portia's mercy speech in *Merchant,* and Katharina's marriage speech in *Taming*). Shakespeare's genius is too comprehensive for the meager labels put on the plays in the eighteenth century.

Others by Shakespeare: *Othello* (play), *Hamlet* (play), and *Macbeth* (play).

Movies: *The Taming of the Shrew* (1967). Franco Zeffirelli, director. Starring Elizabeth Taylor, Richard Burton, and Michael York.
The Taming of the Shrew (1976). Kirk Browning, director. Starring Marc Singer, Harry Hamlin, and Fredi Olster.

Reading Icons:

Title: *Their Eyes Were Watching God*
Author: Zora Neale Hurston
Genre: Novel **Number of Pages:** 193 **Date:** 1937
Level of Challenge: 4
Synopsis:
Janie was a woman with the capacity for joy, in a world that did not see joy as a woman's birthright. *Their Eyes Were Watching God* is the story of Janie's endurance of the social norm, her struggle to find her own life and voice, and her true love for an engaging roustabout named Tea Cake. Along the way, the novel takes a humorous and penetrating look at black culture from Jacksonville, Florida, to the Everglades at the beginning of the twentieth century.

Quotations:
"Now, women forget all those things they don't want to remember, and remember everything they don't want to forget. The dream is the truth. Then they act and do things accordingly." Page 1.

"Lawd have mussy? Dat's de very prong all us black women gits hung on. Dis love! Dat's just whut's got us uh pullin' and uh haulin' and sweatin' and doin' from can't see in de mornin' till can't see at night." Page 23.

"Ah often wonder how dat lil wife uh hisn makes out wid him, 'cause he's uh man dat changes everything, but nothin' don't change him." Page 49.

"Half gods are worshipped in wine and flowers. Real gods require blood." Page 145.

"Two things everybody's got tuh do fuh theyselves. They got tuh go tuh God, and they got tuh find out about livin' fuh theyselves." Page 192.

Reading Hints:
Hurston was a professional anthropologist, studying black folklore and linguistics in Harlem, Florida, Jamaica, and Haiti before writing *Their Eyes Were Watching God*. Readers can see this expertise in her careful attention to dialect, her knowledge of black proverbs, and even her facility with the age

old black tradition of "the Dozens" (a ritual of witty, graceful, and ever escalating insults).

Others by Hurston: *Jonah's Gourd Vine* (novel), *Dust Tracks on a Road* (autobiography), and *The Complete Stories* (short stories).

Reading Icons:

Title: *To Kill a Mockingbird*
Author: Harper Lee
Genre: Novel **Number of Pages:** 284 **Date:** May 1960
Level of Challenge: 4
Synopsis:
A couple of precocious kids, an ethical lawyer, a spurious rape charge, and the high-running racial tensions of the preintegration deep South make this a classic novel and a real page turner. Scout, the narrator, comes of age in the midst of personal, social, and legal turmoil the likes of which most of us have never had to experience.

Quotations:
"Until I feared I would lose it, I never loved to read. One does not love breathing." Page 22.

"Atticus was right. One time he said you never really know a man until you stand in his shoes and walk around in them." Page 282.

"Nigger-lover is just one of those terms that don't mean anything—like snot nose. It's hard to explain—ignorant, trashy people use it when they think somebody's favoring Negroes over and above themselves." Page 113.

Reading Hints:
This book has empathy for everyone: drug addicts, shut-ins, single fathers, blacks, uneducated adults, and wayward children. Remember that empathizing with, and approving of, are two different things.

Another by Lee: This is Lee's only novel. *Matar un Ruisenor* (Spanish translation of *To Kill a Mockingbird*).

Movie: *To Kill a Mockingbird* (1962). Robert Mulligan, director. Starring Gregory Peck, with Robert Duvall as Boo Radley.

Reading Icons:

Title: *The Un-Wedding*
Author: Babette Cole

Genre: Children's Book **Number of Pages:** 32 **Date:** 1997
Level of Challenge: 1 (Reading Ages 4–8)
Synopsis:
Some children's books are surprisingly edgy and deal with adult problems in ways that might make some readers uncomfortable. *The Un-Wedding* is a positive book about divorce that suggests that some parents, and their children, would be better off living happily in two households rather than miserably in one.
Quotations:
"Demetrius and Paula Ogglebutt were two perfectly beautiful children . . . but . . . they had two problem parents who could never agree about anything." Page 1.
"Paula and Demetrius became worried by their parents' behavior. They thought it might be their fault." Page 11.
"So they went to see the minister to ask if he could un-marry their parents." Page 17.
Reading Hints:
Many modern children's books address the peculiar problems of contemporary children. Since half of the marriages in the United States end in divorce, it is clear that many modern children have to deal with issues—like divorce, stepparents, and gay marriages—that former generations were less likely to encounter. Readers will want to select carefully stories that embody the special values and principles that they wish to pass on to their own children.
Others by Cole: *Mummy Laid an Egg* (children's book), *The Bad Good Manners Book* (children's book), and *Drop Dead* (children's book).

Reading Icons:

Title: *The Volcano Lover: A Romance*
Author: Susan Sontag
Genre: Novel **Number of Pages:** 419 **Date:** 1992
Level of Challenge: 4
Synopsis:
In an amazing historical novel, Sontag reimagines, from a postmodern perspective, the infamous affair between Admiral (and Lord) Horatio Nelson and Emma Hamilton, wife of Sir William Hamilton. Sontag is interested in much more than the two lovers, though; her novel explores the worlds of obsessive collection, volcano mania, aesthete philosophy, and that age-old dichotomy between reality and appearances.

Quotations:

"Collectors and curators of collections often admit without too much prodding to misanthropic feelings. They confirm that, yes, they have cared more for inanimate things than for people. . . . You can trust the things. They never change their nature." Page 108.

"The Cavaliere, as besotted with the young admiral in his way as his wife was in hers, looked on fondly." Page 200.

"As one passion begins to fail it is necessary to form another, for the whole art of going through life tolerably is to keep oneself eager about anything." Page 366.

"Women may be vain, but when a man is vain it is beyond believing, for a man is willing to die for his vanity." Page 403.

Reading Hints:

At the end of *The Volcano Lover* a host of new and returning characters speak to the reader directly and give their thoughts about the events in the novel. Readers will need to sort out all those new voices, decide how reliable those voices might be, and then rethink their reading of the novel accordingly.

Others by Sontag: *The Benefactor* (novel), *Death Kit* (novel), and *I, etcetera* (short stories).

Reading Icons:

Title: *Who's Afraid of Virginia Woolf?*
Author: Edward Albee
Genre: Play Script **Number of Pages:** 242 **Date:** 1962
Level of Challenge: 4
Synopsis:

George, a seemingly ineffectual historian, and Martha, his vicious but vulnerable wife, invite a young, new faculty member and his wife over for an after-party drink. In three acts, "Fun and Games," "Walpurgisnacht," and "The Exorcism," Albee exposes both couples for what they really are, in a series of increasingly demeaning and brutal psychological "games."

Quotations:

"The most profound indication of a social malignancy . . . no sense of humor. None of the monoliths could take a joke. Read history. I know something about history." Page 68.

"I stand warned. (Laughs) It's you sneaky types worry me the most, you know. You ineffectual sons of bitches . . . you're the worst." Page 111.

"Oh come on ... let's think of something else. We've played Humiliate the Host. ... We've gone through that one.... What shall we do now?" Page 138. "I'm loud, and I'm vulgar, and I wear the pants in this house because somebody's got to, but I am not a monster. I am not." Page 157.

Reading Hints:
Some playwrights give very few stage directions, but Albee is most helpful in pointing the lines for the actors. Readers should pay special attention to the parenthetical remarks by the author, to see what kind of intonation they should use when they say the lines in their minds. Example: "(Looks about the room. Imitates Bette Davis)," page 3.

Others by Albee: *The Zoo Story* (play), *The Sandbox* (play), and *A Delicate Balance* (play).

Movie: *Who's Afraid of Virginia Woolf?* (1966). Mike Nichols, director. Starring Richard Burton, Elizabeth Taylor, and Sandy Dennis.

Reading Icons:

Title: *Wit*
Author: Margaret Edson
Genre: Play Script **Number of Pages:** 66 **Date:** 1999
Level of Challenge: 4

Synopsis:
Dr. Vivian Bearing is an uncompromising professor and a scholar of seventeenth-century poetry who has quite unexpectedly found herself stricken with stage-four ovarian cancer. She enters the oncology ward of her own university hospital and is treated by a driven and scholarly medical researcher, who was not only one of her own students but in many ways also her intellectual counterpart. Weighing the value of wit and intellectual pursuits against human compassion, both Dr. Bearing and the reader arrive at some surprising and often humorous conclusions.

Quotations:
"One thing can be said for an eight-month course of cancer treatment: it is highly educational. I am learning to suffer." Page 27.

"They read me like a book. Once I did the teaching; now I am taught. This is much easier. I just hold still and look cancerous. It requires less acting every time." Page 32.

"I am not in isolation because I have cancer, because I have a tumor the size of a grapefruit. No. I am in isolation because I am being treated for cancer. My treatment imperils my health." Page 39.

Reading Hints:
Edson has been kind enough to give a number of significant stage directions, each of which is important for fully producing or even imagining the play. Readers will want to pay attention to these directions—for example, "Jason and Kelekian wear lab coats, but each has a different shirt and tie every time he enters. " Why would Edson stress a seemingly small detail of clothing like this? What do the stage directions tell about the meaning of the play?

Another by Edson: *Wit* is her first play. It won a Pulitzer Prize.

Movie: *Wit* (2001). Mike Nichols, director. Starring Emma Thompson, Christopher Lloyd, and Eileen Atkins.

Reading Icons:

Title: *Woman on the Edge of Time*
Author: Marge Piercy
Genre: Novel **Number of Pages:** 381 **Date:** 1976
Level of Challenge: 3
Synopsis:
Is Connie Ramos a garden-variety schizophrenic, driven to madness by living conditions for a thirtyish Chicana, a woman in New York in the 1970s? Or is she a time traveler, able to communicate with a future in which a utopian, agrarian, society is competing for survival with a brutal, technological, totalitarian state? This classic feminist novel has wonderful characters, provocative ideas, and an interesting view of gender relations.

Quotations:
"The first time here, she had been scared of the other patients—violent, crazy, out-of-control animals. She had learned. It was the staff she must watch out for." Page 59.

"But I think we often settle for sex when we want love. And we often want love when we need something else, like a good job or a chance to go back to school." Page 86.

"Connie, we think art is production. We think making a painting is as real as growing a peach or making diving gear. No more real, no less real. It's useful and good on a different level, but it's production." Page 267.

Reading Hints:
There are two alternate futures shown in this novel. One is a utopia (an ideal or perfect society), and the other is a dystopia (a totally debased or flawed society). Readers might like to think about their own ideas of what a per-

fect society would look like. Who would be in charge, what would have value, how would the society create and distribute wealth?

Others by Piercy: *Summer People* (novel), *Gone to Soldiers* (novel), and *Small Changes* (novel).

Reading Icons:

Title: *Wuthering Heights*
Author: Emily Brontë
Genre: Novel **Number of Pages:** 408 **Date:** 1847
Level of Challenge: 4
Synopsis:
Heathcliff and Catherine love with a passion as chilling and compelling as the moors of northern England, where they had been haphazardly reared. Their story confirms that grand passions can breed anywhere, that tragedy is not just for the nobility, and that temperamental natures affect everyone and everything in their path.

Quotations:
"Whatever our souls are made of, his and mine are the same; and Linton's is as different as a moonbeam from lightning, or frost from fire." Page 95.

"Had I been born where laws are less strict and tastes less dainty, I should treat myself to a slow vivisection of those two, as an evening's amusement." Page 325.

"I cannot look down to this floor, but her features are shaped in the flags! Every cloud, in every tree—filling the air at night, and caught by glimpses in every object by day—I am surrounded with her image!" Page 390.

Reading Hints:
The Brontë sisters were raised on a diet of Shakespeare and the Bible, and their familiarity with both shows in all of their novels. *Wuthering Heights* shares one of the stronger themes of Shakespeare's *As You Like It:* the consequences of unfair treatment among brothers. Readers will probably also enjoy noticing echoes of *Hamlet, Lear,* and the sonnets in *Wuthering Heights.*

Another by Brontë: This is Emily Brontë's first and only novel.

Movies: *Wuthering Heights* (1939). William Wyler, director. Starring Lawrence Olivier, Merle Oberon, and David Niven.

Wuthering Heights (1970). Robert Fuest, director. Starring Anna Calder-Marshall, Timothy Dalton, and Harry Andrews.

Reading Icons:

Title: *You Never Know: A Legend of the Lamed-vavniks*
Author: Francine Prose and Mark Podwal (illustrator)
Genre: Children's Book **Number of Pages:** 24 **Date:** 1998
Level of Challenge: 1 (Reading Ages 4–8)
Synopsis:
This is the story of Schmuel the Shoemaker of Plotchnik, a *Lamed-vavnik,* one of the thirty-six holy people who inhabit the earth in every generation, whose prayers go straight to God, because they are so humble, just, and kind. Schmuel is not very highly regarded by the villagers of Plotchnik until a great drought and then a great deluge call his special gifts into play. It turns out that everyone deserves respect, even the folks who seem most unlikely.
Quotations:
"For forty days and forty nights no rain fell on the town of Plotchnik." Page 1.
"Whenever there was trouble, somehow Schmuel was—magically!—always
     right there, ready to help." Page 5.
"Why does God listen to Poor Schmuel and not to us?" Page 10.
Reading Hints:
The *Lamed-vavnik*s are characters from the Jewish tradition. Many children's stories tell ancient religious stories in a way that children can understand. Whether the tradition is Islamic, Christian, Jewish, or Hindu, the lessons of these stories are usually universal and admired by any person who cares about good and evil, or right and wrong behavior. Readers enjoying this book with a child should have a lot of fun saying words like "Schmuel," "Plotchnik," and *"Lamed-vavnik."*
Others by Prose: *Hunters and Gatherers* (novel), *Dybbuk: A Story Made in Heaven* (children's book), and *Household Saints* (novel).

Reading Icons:

III

BECOMING A BOOK JUNKIE

6

ACTIVE READING

*A*ctive reading requires readers to think while they read, not passively accept the words on the page but engaging them in a dialog: questioning, amplifying, emending, agreeing, and disagreeing with the ideas expressed. The most renowned advocate of active reading began his quest to bring art, philosophy, reading skills, and the "Great Books" to America in the 1920s. Anyone who reads today cannot help but be impressed by his definitive essay, "How to Mark a Book." Mortimer J. Adler—professor, philosopher, and educational theorist—still has the last and best word on how to approach the books that matter. Readers who follow his sage advice will find the suggested reading journal in the next section of Book Savvy all the more easy, enjoyable, and meaningful.

"HOW TO MARK A BOOK," BY MORTIMER J. ADLER

You know you have to read "between the lines" to get the most out of anything. I want to persuade you to do something equally important in the course of your reading. I want to persuade you to write between the lines. Unless you do, you are not likely to do the most efficient kind of reading.

I contend, quite bluntly, that marking up a book is not an act of mutilation but of love. You shouldn't mark up a book which isn't yours.

Librarians (or your friends) who lend you books expect you to keep them clean, and you should. If you decide that I am right about the usefulness of marking books, you will have to buy them. Most of the world's great books are available today, in reprint editions.

There are two ways in which one can own a book. The first is the property right you establish by paying for it, just as you pay for clothes and furniture. But this act of purchase is only the prelude to possession. Full ownership comes only when you have made it a part of yourself, and the best way to make yourself a part of it is by writing in it. An illustration may make the point clear. You buy a beefsteak and transfer it from the butcher's icebox to your own. But you do not own the beefsteak in the most important sense until you consume it and get it into your bloodstream. I am arguing that books, too, must be absorbed into your bloodstream to do you any good.

Confusion about what it means to "own" a book leads people to a false reverence for paper, binding, and type—a respect for the physical thing—the craft of the printer rather than the genius of the author. They forget that it is possible for a man to acquire the idea, to possess the beauty, which a great book contains, without staking his claim by pasting his bookplate inside the cover. Having a fine library doesn't prove that its owner has a mind enriched by books; it proves nothing more than that he, his father, or his wife, was rich enough to buy them.

There are three kinds of book owners. The first has all the standard sets and best sellers—unread, untouched. (This deluded individual owns wood pulp and ink, not books.) The second has a great many books—a few of them read through, most of them dipped into, but all of them as clean and shiny as the day they were bought. (This person would probably like to make books his own, but is restrained by a false respect for their physical appearance.) The third has a few books or many—every one of them dog-eared and dilapidated, shaken and loosened by continual use, marked and scribbled in from front to back. (This man owns books.)

Is it false respect, you may ask, to preserve intact and unblemished a beautifully printed book, an elegantly bound edition? Of course not. I'd no more scribble all over a first edition of *Paradise Lost* than I'd give my baby a set of crayons and an original Rembrandt. I wouldn't mark up a painting or a statue. Its soul, so to speak, is inseparable from its body. And the beauty of a rare edition or of a richly manufactured volume is like that of a painting or a statue.

But the soul of a book "can" be separate from its body. A book is more like the score of a piece of music than it is like a painting. No great musician confuses a symphony with the printed sheets of music. Arturo Toscanini reveres Brahms, but Toscanini's score of the G-minor Symphony is so thoroughly marked up that no one but the maestro himself can read it. The reason why a great conductor makes notations on his musical scores—marks them up again and again each time he returns to study them—is the reason why you should mark your books. If your respect for magnificent binding or typography gets in the way, buy yourself a cheap edition and pay your respects to the author.

Why is marking up a book indispensable to reading? First, it keeps you awake. (And I don't mean merely conscious; I mean awake.) In the second place; reading, if it is active, is thinking, and thinking tends to express itself in words, spoken or written. The marked book is usually the thought-through book. Finally, writing helps you remember the thoughts you had, or the thoughts the author expressed. Let me develop these three points.

If reading is to accomplish anything more than passing time, it must be active. You can't let your eyes glide across the lines of a book and come up with an understanding of what you have read. Now an ordinary piece of light fiction, like, say, *Gone With the Wind,* doesn't require the most active kind of reading. The books you read for pleasure can be read in a state of relaxation, and nothing is lost. But a great book, rich in ideas and beauty, a book that raises and tries to answer great fundamental questions, demands the most active reading of which you are capable. You don't absorb the ideas of John Dewey the way you absorb the crooning of Mr. [Rudy] Vallee [popular singer]. You have reach for them. That you cannot do while you're asleep.

If, when you've finished reading a book, the pages are filled with your notes, you know that you read actively. The most famous "active" reader of great books I know is President Hutchins, of the University of Chicago. He also has the hardest schedule of business activities of any man I know. He invariably reads with a pencil, and sometimes, when he picks up a book and pencil in the evening, he finds himself, instead of making intelligent notes, drawing what he calls "caviar factories" on the margins. When that happens, he puts the book down. He knows he's too tired to read, and he's just wasting time.

But, you may ask, why is writing necessary? Well, the physical act of writing, with your own hand, brings words and sentences more sharply before your mind and preserves them better in your memory. To set down your reaction to important words and sentences you have read, and the questions they have raised in your mind, is to preserve those reactions and sharpen those questions.

Even if you wrote on a scratch pad, and threw the paper away when you had finished writing, your grasp of the book would be surer. But you don't have to throw the paper away. The margins (top and bottom, as well as sides), the end-papers, the very space between the lines, are all available. They aren't sacred. And, best of all, your marks and notes become an integral part of the book and stay there forever. You can pick up the book the following week or year, and there are all your points of agreement, disagreement, doubt, and inquiry. It's like resuming an interrupted conversation with the advantage of being able to pick up where you left off.

And that is exactly what reading a book should be: a conversation between you and the author. Presumably he knows more about the subject than you do; naturally, you'll have the proper humility as you approach him. But don't let anybody tell you that a reader is supposed to be solely on the receiving end. Understanding is a two-way operation; learning doesn't consist in being an empty receptacle. The learner has to question himself and question the teacher. He even has to argue with the teacher, once he understands what the teacher is saying. And marking a book is literally an expression of differences, or agreements of opinion, with the author.

There are all kinds of devices for marking a book intelligently and fruitfully. Here's the way I do it:

- *Underlining (or highlighting):* of major points, of important or forceful statements.
- *Vertical lines at the margin:* to emphasize a statement already underlined.
- *Star, asterisk, or other doo-dad at the margin:* to be used sparingly, to emphasize the ten or twenty most important statements in the book. (You may want to fold the bottom corner of each page on which you use such marks. It won't hurt the sturdy paper on which most modern books are printed, and you will be able take the book off the shelf at any time and, by opening it at the folded-corner page, refresh your recollection of the book.)
- *Numbers in the margin:* to indicate the sequence of points the author makes in developing a single argument.
- *Numbers of other pages in the margin:* to indicate where else in the book the author made points relevant to the point marked; to tie up the ideas in a book, which, though they may be separated by many pages, belong together.
- *Circling or highlighting of key words or phrases.*
- *Writing in the margin, or at the top or bottom of the page,* for the sake of: recording questions (and perhaps answers) which a passage raised in your mind; reducing a complicated discussion to a simple statement; recording the sequence of major points right through the book. I use the end-papers at the back of the book to make a personal index of the author's points in the order of their appearance.

The front end-papers are to me the most important. Some people reserve them for a fancy bookplate. I reserve them for fancy thinking. After I have finished reading the book and making my personal index on the back end-papers, I turn to the front and try to outline the book, not page by page or point by point (I've already done that at the back), but as an integrated structure, with a basic unity and an order of parts. This outline is, to me, the measure of my understanding of the work.

If you're a die-hard anti-book-marker, you may object that the margins, the space between the lines, and the end-papers don't give you room enough. All right. How about using a scratch pad slightly smaller than the page-size of the book—so that the edges of the sheets won't protrude? Make your index, outlines and even your notes on the pad, and then insert these sheets permanently inside the front and back covers of the book.

Or, you may say that this business of marking books is going to slow up your reading. It probably will. That's one of the reasons for doing it. Most of us have been taken in by the notion that speed of reading is a measure of our intelligence. There is no such thing as the right speed for intelligent reading. Some things should be read quickly and effortlessly and some should be read slowly and even laboriously. The sign of intelligence in reading is the ability to read different things differently according to their worth. In the case of good books, the point is not to see how many of them you can get through, but rather how many can get through you—how many you can make your own. A few friends are better than a thousand acquaintances. If this be your aim, as it should be, you will not be impatient if it takes more time and effort to read a great book than it does a newspaper.

You may have one final objection to marking books. You can't lend them to your friends because nobody else can read them without being distracted by your notes. Furthermore, you won't want to lend them because a marked copy is a kind of intellectual diary, and lending it is almost like giving your mind away.

If your friend wishes to read your *Plutarch's Lives, Shakespeare,* or *The Federalist Papers,* tell him gently but firmly, to buy a copy. You will lend him your car or your coat—but your books are as much a part of you as your head or your heart.

7

DEVELOPING A READING JOURNAL

WHAT IS A READING JOURNAL?

The word "journal" comes from the French word for day *(jour)*; the original meaning was a diary in which a person would write down his or her thoughts daily. Today, people use journals as private places to assemble their thoughts on a variety of topics: gardening journals, records of public events, travel diaries, close observations of scientific results, spiritual memoirs, or even ideas for products, inventions, or songs. People rarely have the time to write in their journals everyday anymore, so they simply go to their journals when they have the time and the spirit moves them.

A reading journal is a private place where readers assemble their thoughts and feelings about the books that they are currently reading. When it comes to the journal itself, some journal writers like the sensual pleasure of a fancy leather binding and the flow of jet-black ink from a fine fountain pen on crème laid paper; while others like the freedom and expressiveness of an inexpensive, dime-store composition book scribbled in with whatever writing tool is at hand. A reading journal can even be a designated file folder on a computer desktop, although most journal writers find blank books, drawing pads, three-ring binders, or anything else that they can carry around and keep with their books more convenient. There are really only two important things to remember when selecting a journal to write in: pens are more archival than pencils, and computer files have to be backed up regularly. Reading journals are meant to last a lifetime.

Also, consider that many writers enjoy drawing, making charts, painting pictures, creating maps, or doodling in their journals. The journal is their private place to be creative and imaginative.

WHY KEEP A READING JOURNAL?

- Any book that is worth reading is worth thinking and writing about.
- Reading journals help readers keep a record of their important first impressions.
- Reading journals help readers focus and reflect on what they have read.
- Reading journals help to integrate the reading and writing processes.
- Reading journals sharpen thinking and improve writing skills.
- Reading journals help readers generate new ideas and content for their own writing.
- Reading journals help readers save important quotes and meaningful passages from their reading.
- Reading journals help readers trace their attitudes and aptitudes through time.
- Reading journals preserve a record of the reader's intellectual, emotional, and spiritual growth.
- Reading journals help readers share their reading experiences with others.
- Reading journals help readers keep track of their favorite authors.
- Reading journals help readers emulate the authors who mean the most to them.
- Reading journals are fun.

READING JOURNAL PROMPTS

Most writers find it helpful to put certain information in the heading of their reading journal entry. This might include data like:

The name of the author
The title of the book
The genre
The date of publication
The publisher
The date started and completed
Where the book was found
A rating system (10 = everyone has to read this book; 1 = no one should have to read it).

Most writers also find it useful to have a set of writing prompts to help them get started with their writing—certain questions they can ask themselves that invariably stimulate interesting ideas and perceptions. Readers who do not already have such a set of questions ready-made might like to select some of the following for their reading journals. Readers will want to answer the questions that interest them and leave the rest behind.

- What made me select this book in the first place?
- Did the book meet my expectations for fun, suspense, information, or whatever else I was looking for?
- Did the characters in this book remind me of anyone I know?
- Were there any words in the book that I wanted to look up and remember so that I could add them to my working vocabulary?
- What other book, or books, does this book remind me of, and why?
- Did I recognize any interesting patterns in the book—for example, images, gestures, characters, songs, or colors?
- What aspects of the writer's style would I like to be able to imitate in my own writing? What aspects did I hate?
- Was there anything I knew about the author's real life that seemed to have a bearing on the way this book was written?
- If I could write a letter to the author of this book, what would I like to say to him or her, or what would I like to ask?
- Were there any memorable quotations, stories, or examples that I particularly want to remember from this book?
- Who told the story in this book, and would it have made a difference if another character, or someone else entirely, had told the story?
- What was the most confusing aspect of this book for me?
- How does this book relate to my life—in the past, now, and in the future?
- What were my feelings when I finished this book?
- What was the single most important thing I believe this author wanted me to understand from reading the book?
- What are the three most important things to me that I learned from reading this book?
- Can I write a one-paragraph synopsis of the book that would help someone else decide whether they want to read it or not?
- To whom else would I recommend this book and why?

SAMPLE READING JOURNAL ANSWERS

Journal writers are usually less concerned about "correctness" than in getting their ideas down on paper. When answering their own prompts, they tend to look at the questions loosely, letting the answers take them wherever they want. Since reading journals are usually saved and savored for years, it is useful to be as specific as possible when writing in them and to write or print clearly. Things written in a journal today can often provide the spark for a bit of public writing years later.

Here are a few typical responses to the sample writing prompts given earlier:

What Made Me Select This Book in the First Place?

Over the years, a number of my good friends who knew that I had not had the opportunity to read as a child, recommended Burnett's *The Secret Garden* to me. Each of them seemed to have a special relationship with the book: One was fascinated with the idea of being an orphan, another liked the notion of a secret enclosed space, and still another thought it was a wonderful story of childhood friendship. I had to read the book to find out why all the people I loved remembered it so fondly.

Did I Recognize Any Interesting Patterns in the Book? Was I Struck, for Example, by Images, Gestures, Characters, Songs, or Colors?

I think I would have had a difficult time understanding Flannery O'Connor's short story "A Good Man Is Hard to Find" if she hadn't repeated the title several times during the story. The Misfit is certainly not anyone's idea of a good man, and yet O'Connor's Christian charity obviously extends even to him. It makes one think twice about judging others from the outside.

Who Told the Story in This Book, and Would It Have Made a Difference If Another Character, or Someone Else Entirely, Had Told the Story?

Nabakov's *Lolita* is told by Humbert Humbert, the highly educated, articulate, European, child molester. From inside his mind, it is clear that he loved Lolita and that he did not want to harm her. But I can imagine it would have been a very different story if told by Lolita in her teenage slang, with her childish sophistication and her very real pain and anguish.

What Aspects of the Writer's Style Would I Like to be Able to Imitate in My Own Writing? What Aspects Did I Hate?

Henry James can really write a long sentence and keep control of it. I noticed that he was able to do this by using punctuation that I hardly ever use. I can see that semicolons are quite useful for putting related ideas together in the same sentence. On the other hand, he sometimes overdoes it. I think some of his sentences would have been clearer if he had "divided and conquered."

How Does This Book Relate to My Life—in the Past, Now, and in the Future?

This play, *Wit,* about a college English professor dying of cancer, really hit close to home. She was an excellent teacher but sometimes a bit too focused on her subject matter, rather than on her students. It made me think back to the times when I might have been a bit gentler with students who were troubled and failing, and it makes me want to be even more patient with my present students. It also makes it clear to me that I want to teach fewer classes in the future and spend more of the last years of my career writing books.

To Whom Would I Recommend This Book and Why?

I think I'll give my copy of Michener's *Alaska* to my friend Chris. It's not a book that I want to read again, but it was full of information about the state, from its formation to the present. I think she'll find it useful on her two-week cruise up the Inside Passage next month. If I ever go to Alaska, I want to make sure to remember to visit Sitka and Denali National Park.

The prompts are just a way of getting started. Every book is different, and every entry in a reading journal has its own special logic and character. Journals don't get kept if they are a chore, so make it an enjoyable activity, in any way that works.

APPENDIX A:
BOOK LISTS AND AWARDS

Books, or authors, in the following lists that are featured in Book Savvy *will be followed by the notation:* **Savvy**

There are prestigious book lists and literature awards for nearly every kind of writing: novels, poetry, short stories, plays, children's books, mysteries, gay fiction, horror stories, humor, westerns, and fantasy. There is even a Nobel Prize in Literature. The awards vary from the teapot with skull-and-crossbones given by the Agatha Awards to the thirty-two-thousand-dollar prize for the Man Booker Prize for Fiction. Pulitzer Prize winners get a surprisingly small five-thousand-dollar award, but the roll-on publicity and benefits of a Pulitzer are of inestimable value in a writer's career. Some awards are national and include only works written originally in English; others are international in scope and include works written in many other languages.

Here are some examples of famous book lists and their recent winners. These book lists and awards are excellent places for readers to browse when searching for their next good book. One thing to notice is the variety of the winners, from list to list. Each organization has its own criteria for judging books and its own way of selecting its annual winners. Many of the lists are annotated, as the one in this book is, and many are not. Readers wanting more information about any book they find on an unannotated list simply have to plug the exact title into their favorite search engine to turn up notices, reviews, and even sales and remainder copies. *Google, Alta Vista, Ixquick* metasearch, *and Yahoo!* are all good places to start.

THE AGATHA AWARDS

This award is given at the annual convention of *Malice Domestic* to the best mystery novel published in the United States by a living author in the previous year, as exemplified by Agatha Christie's novels (no excessive violence, an amateur detective, a confined setting, and characters who know each other). Visit www.malicedomestic.org/agatha.htm.
Murphy's Law; A Molly Murphy Mystery by Rhys Bowen. 2001. **Savvy**
Storm Track by Margaret Maron. 2000.
Mariner's Compass by Earlene Fowler. 1999.
Butcher's Hill by Laura Lippman. 1998.
The Devil in Music by Kate Ross. 1997.

AMERICAN LIBRARY ASSOCIATION GLBT AWARDS

This award is given by a unit of the American Library Association for books that explore gay, lesbian, bisexual, or transgendered themes. Visit www .literature-awards.com/american_library_association_glbtrt.htm.
The Laramie Project by Moises Kaufman/TectonicTheatre Project. 2002.
Affinity by Sarah Waters. 2001.
Po Man's Child: A Novel by Marci Blackman. 2000.
The Hours by Michael Cunningham. 1999. **Savvy**
Working Parts: A Novel by Lucy Jane Bledsoe. 1998.

ARTHUR C. CLARKE AWARD

This award honors the best science fiction novel published in Britain during the previous year. Visit www.lsi.usp.br/~rbianchi/clarke/ACC.Award.html.
Bold as Love by Gwyneth Jones. 2002.
Perdido Street Station by China Miéville. 2001.
Distraction by Bruce Sterling. 2000.
Dreaming in Smoke by Tricia Sullivan. 1999.
The Sparrow by Mary Doria Russell. 1998.

THE BAD SEX IN FICTION AWARDS

This award was created by The Literary Review for the worst, most redundant, or embarrassing description of physical joining in a novel. Visit www.literature-awards.com/bad_sex_in_fiction_award.htm.

Tread Softly by Wendy Perriam. 2002.
Rescue Me by Christopher Hart. 2001.
Kissing England by Sean Thomas. 2000.
Starcrossed by A. A. Gill. 1999.
Charlotte Gray by Sebastian Faulks. 1998.

THE BRAM STOKER AWARDS

The Bram Stoker Award, named for the author of the novel *Dracula,* is presented by the Horror Writer's Association for a work of horror fiction written in English and published in the previous year. Visit www.horror.org/stokers.htm.
American Gods by Neil Gaiman. 2001. **Savvy**
The Traveling Vampire Show by Richard Laymon. 2000.
Mr. X by Peter Straub. 1999.
Bag of Bones by Stephen King. 1998.
Children of the Dusk by Janet Berliner and George Guthridge. 1997.

THE CALDECOTT MEDAL

This award is given by the Association for Library Service to Children to the artist of the most distinguished American picture book for children. Visit www.ala.org/Content/NavigationMenu/ALSC/Awards_and_Scholarships1/Literary_and_Related_Awards/Caldecott_Medal/Caldecott_Medal.html.
My Friend Rabbit by author/illustrator Eric Rohmann. 2003.
The Three Pigs by David Wiesner. 2002.
So You Want to Be President? Illustrated by David Small; text by Judith St. George. 2001.
Joseph Had a Little Overcoat by Simms Taback. 2000.
Snowflake Bentley. Illustrated by Mary Azarian; text by Jacqueline Briggs Martin. 1999.

THE HUGO AWARDS

This award is given by the World Science Fiction Society to a work of science fiction, voted on by their membership, published in the previous calendar year. Visit worldcon.org/hugos.html.

American Gods by Neil Gaiman. 2002. **Savvy**
Harry Potter and the Goblet of Fire by J. K. Rowling. 2001. **Savvy**
A Deepness in the Sky by Vernor Vinge. 2000.
To Say Nothing of the Dog by Connie Willis. 1999.
forever peace by Joe Haldeman. 1998. **Savvy**

THE MAN BOOKER PRIZE FOR FICTION

This award aims to reward the best novel of the year written in English by a citizen of the Commonwealth or Republic of Ireland. Visit www.booker prize.co.uk/.
Life of Pi by Yann Martel. 2002.
True History of the Kelly Gang by Peter Carey. 2001.
The Blind Assassin by Margaret Atwood. 2000. **Savvy**
Disgrace by J. M. Coetzee. 1999.
Amsterdam: A Novel by Ian McEwan. 1998.

THE MODERN LIBRARY LIST: HUNDRED BEST NOVELS

Here are the top five of the hundred best English-language novels of the twentieth century as drawn up by the editorial board of the Modern Library. Visit www.randomhouse.com/modernlibrary/100best.html.
Ulysses by James Joyce.
The Great Gatsby by F. Scott Fitzgerald.
A Portrait of the Artist as a Young Man by James Joyce.
Lolita by Vladimir Nabokov. **Savvy**
Brave New World by Aldous Huxley. **Savvy**

THE MODERN LIBRARY READERS' LIST: HUNDRED BEST NOVELS

Here are the top five of the hundred best English-language novels of the twentieth century as chosen by the readers of the Modern Library series. Visit www.randomhouse.com/modernlibrary/100bestnovels.html.
igged by Ayn Rand.
tainhead by Ayn Rand.

Battlefield Earth by L. Ron Hubbard.
The Lord of the Rings by J. R. R. Tolkien.
To Kill a Mockingbird by Harper Lee. *Savvy*

THE NEBULA AWARDS

This award is given by the Science Fiction Writers of America to acknowledge excellence in science fiction writing. Visit dpsinfo.com/awardweb/nebulas/.
American Gods by Neil Gaiman. 2002. *Savvy*
The Quantum Rose by Catherine Asara. 2001.
Darwin's Radio by Greg Bear. 2000.
Parable of the Talents by Octavia E. Butler. 1999.
forever peace by Joe Haldeman. 1998. *Savvy*

THE NOBEL PRIZE FOR LITERATURE

This award is given by the Swedish Academy for a distinguished lifetime of achievement in literature. Visit almaz.com/nobel/literature/literature.html.
Imre Kertész, Hungary. 2002. *Savvy*
V. S. Naipaul, Great Britain. 2001.
Gao Xingjian, China. 2000. *Savvy*
Gunter Grass, Germany. 1999.
Jose Saramago, Portugal. 1998.

OPRAH'S BOOK CLUB LIST

Oprah's Book Club selections are books that are well written, pleasurable to read, and deal intelligently and tenderly with the human condition. Visit www.oprah.com/books/books_landing.jhtml;jsessionid=YL1I4VP-MEBD2LLARAYHCFEQ.
Sula by Toni Morrison. April 2002.
Fall on Your Knees by Anne-Marie MacDonald. January 2002.
A Fine Balance by Robinton Mistry. November 2001.
The Corrections by Jonathan Franzen. September 2001. *Savvy*
Cane River by Lalita Tademy. June 2001.

PEN/FAULKNER AWARDS

This award is a national prize, named after author William Faulkner, that honors the best published works of fiction by American citizens in a calendar year. Visit www.literature-awards.com/pen_faulkner_award.htm.
The Human Stain by Philip Roth. 2001. ***Savvy***
Waiting by Ha Jin. 2000.
The Hours by Michael Cunningham. 1999. ***Savvy***
The Bear Comes Home by Rafi Zabor. 1998.
Women in Their Beds by Gina Berriault. 1997.

PEN/HEMINGWAY AWARDS

This award is given by the Ernest Hemingway Foundation to an American author who has not previously published a book of fiction. Visit www.literature-awards.com/ernest_hemingway_foundation.htm.
Mary and O'Neil by Justin Cronin. 2001.
An Obedient Father by Akhil Sharma. 2000.
Interpreter of Maladies: Stories by Jhumpa Lahiri. 1999. ***Savvy***
Homestead by Rosina Lippi. 1998.
A Private State by Charlotte Bacon. 1997.

POWELL'S BOOKSTORE LIST
OF TWENTY-FIVE GREAT NOVELS

The staff of Powell's Bookstore, one of the largest bookstores in the world, replied to the Modern Library List with this list of its own favorite novels. Here are its top five. Visit www.powells.com.
Their Eyes Were Watching God by Zora Neale Hurston. ***Savvy***
Beloved by Toni Morrison.
Blood Meridian by Cormac McCormack.
To Kill a Mockingbird by Harper Lee. ***Savvy***
The Color Purple by Alice Walker. ***Savvy***

THE PULITZER PRIZE FOR FICTION

This award is given by the Pulitzer Prize Board for distinguished fiction by an American author, preferably dealing with American life. Visit www .pulitzer.org/year.

Middlesex by Jeffrey Eugenides. 2003.
Empire Falls by Richard Russo. 2002.
The Amazing Adventures of Kavalier & Clay by Michael Chabon. 2001.
Interpreter of Maladies by Jhumpa Lahiri. 2000. **Savvy**
The Hours by Michael Cunningham. 1999. **Savvy**

A complete list of over two hundred Literature Awards winners can be found on the Internet at J. M. McElligott's excellent site: www.literature awards.com/.

APPENDIX B: MORE QUOTATIONS ABOUT BOOKS AND READING

"Most books, indeed, are records less of fullness than of emptiness." —William Allingham

"Books are quiet. They do not dissolve into wavy lines or snowstorm effects. They do not pause to deliver commercials. They are three-dimensional, having length, breadth and depth. They are convenient to handle and completely portable."—Anonymous

"Tell me what you read and I shall tell you what you are."—Anonymous Proverb

"A book is like a garden carried in the pocket."—Arab Proverb

"A real book is not one that's read, but one that reads us."—W. H. Auden

"Some books are to be tasted, others to be swallowed, and some few to be chewed and digested."—Sir Francis Bacon

"People read for amusement. If a book be capable of yielding amusement, it will naturally be read; for no man is an enemy to what gives him pleasure."—James Beattie

"We read not only because we cannot know enough people, but because friendship is so vulnerable, so likely to diminish or disappear, overcome by space, time, imperfect sympathies, and all the sorrows of familial and passional life."—Harold Bloom

"[Reading is like] the sex act—done privately, and often in bed."—Daniel J. Boorstin

"A good reader is rarer than a good writer."—Jorge Luis Borges

"A book that we love haunts us forever; it will haunt us even when we can no longer find it on the shelf or beside the bed where we must have left it."—Editors, *Brick: A Literary Journal*

"There are worse crimes than burning books. One of them is not reading them."—Joseph Brodsky

"It is well to read everything of something, and something of everything."—Henry Brougham

"The practice of fiction can be dangerous; it puts ideas into the head of the world."—Anthony Burgess

"To read without reflecting, is like eating without digesting."—Edmund Burke

"Books are like imprisoned souls till someone takes them down from a shelf and frees them."—Samuel Butler

"History has shown that the less people read, the more books they buy."—Albert Camus

"Reading a book is like re-writing it for yourself. . . . You bring to a novel, anything you read, all your experience of the world. You bring your history and you read it in your own terms."—Angela Carter

"If only I could manage, without annoyance to my family, to get imprisoned for 10 years, 'without hard labour,' and with the use of books and writing materials, it would be simply delightful!"—Lewis Carroll

"There's no book so bad that something good may not be found in it."—Cervantes

"The reading public is intellectually adolescent at best, and it is obvious that what is called 'significant literature' will only be sold to this public by exactly the same methods as are used to sell it toothpaste, cathartics and automobiles."—Raymond Chandler

"It is chiefly through books that we enjoy intercourse with superior minds. . . . In the best books, great men talk to us, give us their most precious thoughts, and pour their souls into ours."—William Ellery Channing

"Achilles exists only through Homer. Take away the art of writing from this world, and you will probably take away all its glory."—Chateaubriand

"There are no new ideas,/Only those which rhyme with certain classics."—Lu Chi

"In books one finds golden mansions and women as beautiful as jewels."—Chinese Proverb

"It's a good thing for an uneducated man to read books of quotations." —Sir Winston Churchill

"To add a library to a house is to give that house a soul."—Cicero

"Some read to think, these are rare; some to write, these are common; and some read to talk, and these form the great majority."—C. C. Colton

"Reading gives us someplace to go when we have to stay where we are."—Mason Cooley

"When young, I longed for someone who would talk to me and, often as not, that person was found in a book. Voices as distinct as any physically present really were there."—Robert Creeley

"A truly great book should be read in youth, again in maturity and once more in old age, as a fine building should be seen by morning light, at noon and by moonlight."—Robertson Davies

"Books should to one of these four ends conduce,/For wisdom, piety, delight, or use."—John Denham

"Whoever has read the best books has acquired not only information but a method of thinking."—Ernest Dimnet

"It is a great thing to start life with a small number of really good books which are your very own."—Sir Arthur Conan Doyle

"Never judge a book by its movie."—J. W. Eagan

"Books are the quietest and most constant of friends; they are the most accessible and wisest of counsellors, and the most patient of teachers."—Charles W. Eliot

"There are books . . . which take rank in your life with parents and lovers and passionate experiences, so medicinal, so stringent, so revolutionary, so authoritative."—Ralph Waldo Emerson

"It is hard to stretch a small vocabulary to make it do all the things that intelligent people require of words. It's like trying to plan a series of menus from the limited resources of a poverty-stricken, war torn country compared to planning such a series in a prosperous, stable country. Words are one of our chief means of adjusting to all the situations of life. The better control we have over words, the more successful our adjustment is likely to be."—Bergen Evans

"When I get a little money, I buy books; if any is left, I buy food and clothes."—Erasmus

"Books are not rolls, to be devoured only when they are hot and fresh. A good book retains its interior heat and will warm a generation yet unborn."—Clifton Fadiman

"I knew David Copperfield better than anybody I knew in the real world, including myself." —Shelby Foote

"The man who is too busy to read is never likely to lead."—B. C. Forbes

"Only two classes of books are of universal appeal: the very best and the very worst."—Ford Madox Ford

"The only books that influence us are those for which we are ready, and which have gone a little farther down our particular path than we have yet got ourselves."—E. M. Forster

"Either write something worth reading or do something worth writing." —Ben Franklin

"If books were Persian carpets, one would not look only at the outer side . . . because it is the stitch that makes a carpet wear, gives it its life and bloom."—Rumer Godden

"Books should not be replaced by anything, by TV or any such thing, because books make it possible to think more deeply."—Mikhail Gorbachev

"To teach people to read without teaching them not to believe everything they read is only to prepare them for a new slavery."—Jean Guehenno

"[Books] give a house character and meaning. The discerning eye looks for them in its first appraisal; their absence is a negative finding upon the cultivation and intelligence of the household."—Helen Haines

"The art of reading is to skip judiciously."—Philip G. Hamerton

"We're the rememberers of the tribe. That's what the tribe hires us for. They say, 'You remember. I'm too busy.'"—Pete Hamill

"Reading silently is like digesting food; no one can do it for you."—Julie Harris

"Wherever they burn books, they will also, in the end, burn human beings."—Heinrich Heine

"All good books are alike in that they are truer than if they had really happened."—Ernest Hemingway

"The novel, in its best form, I regard as one of the most powerful engines of civilization ever invented."—Sir John Frederick Herschel

"All our days we are being fed, often forcibly fed, the mush of group opinion, until many of us long to get our teeth into the honest-to-God thoughts and feelings of a single, specific person. That is what we do when we read a serious novel."—Granville Hicks

"Life-transforming ideas have always come to me through books."—Bell Hooks

"It felt real: I have no higher praise for word on paper."—Isabel Huggan

"Reading is not a duty, and if it is not a pleasure it is a waste of time."—Holbrook Jackson

"The only obligation to which in advance we may hold a novel, without incurring the accusation of being arbitrary, is that it be interesting."—Henry James

"I cannot live without books."—Thomas Jefferson

"The greatest part of a writer's time is spent in reading, in order to write; a man will turn over half a library to make one book."—Samuel Johnson

"A book must be the axe for the frozen sea within us."—Franz Kafka

"Experts generally agree that taking all opportunities to read books and other material aloud to children is the best preparation for their learning to read. The pleasures of being read to are far more likely to strengthen a child's desire to learn to read than are repetitions of sounds, alphabet drills, and deciphering uninteresting words."—Lillian G. Katz

"Literature is my Utopia. Here I am not disfranchised. No barrier of the senses shuts me out from the sweet, gracious discourse of my book friends. They talk to me without embarrassment or awkwardness."—Helen Keller

"To sit alone in the lamplight with a book spread out before you, and hold intimate converse with men of unseen generations—such is a pleasure beyond compare."—Yoshida Kenko

"Beware of the man of one book."—Latin Proverb

"To me, nothing can be more important than giving children books. It's better to be giving books to children than drug treatment to them when they're 15 years old. Did it ever occur to anyone that if you put nice libraries in public schools you wouldn't have to put them in prisons?"—Fran Lebowitz

"The unread story is not a story; it is little black marks on wood pulp. The reader, reading it, makes it live."—Ursula K. Le Guin

"There is only one way to read, which is to browse in libraries and bookshops, picking up books that attract you, reading only those, dropping them when they bore you, skipping the parts that drag—and never, never reading anything because you feel you ought, or because it is part of a trend or a movement. Remember that the book which bores you when you are twenty or thirty will open doors for you when you are forty or fifty—and vice versa. Don't read a book out of its right time for you."—Doris Lessing

"The one fault of really good books is that they almost always produce a great prodigy of bad ones."—G. C. Lichtenberg

"The things I want to know are in books; my best friend is the man who'll get me a book I ain't read."—Abraham Lincoln

"I can imagine living without food. I cannot imagine living without books."—Alice Foote MacDougall

"Reading fiction is a way of finding out about other people—of being with an enormous variety of people in all kinds of circumstances. If you haven't read Dostoevski you haven't been into his strange part of the human soul and I think you're somewhat deprived."—Robert McNeil

"I'm going to introduce a resolution to have the postmaster general stop reading dirty books and deliver the mail."—Senator Gale W. McGee

"I would rather be a poor man in a garret with plenty of books than a king who did not love reading."—Thomas B. Macaulay

"Writing books is the closest men ever come to childbearing."—Norman Mailer

"Something in the relationship between a reader and a book is recognized as wise and fruitful, but it is also seen as disdainfully exclusive and excluding, perhaps because the image of an individual curled up in a corner, seemingly oblivious of the grumblings of the world, suggests impenetrable privacy and a selfish eye and singular secretive action."—Alberto Manguel

"In literature as in love, we are astonished at what is chosen by others."—Andre Maurois

"Some time ago a publisher told me that there are four kinds of books that seldom, if ever, lose money in the United States—first, murder stories; secondly, novels in which the heroine is forcibly overcome by the hero; thirdly, volumes on spiritualism, occultism and other such claptrap; and fourthly, books on Lincoln."—H. L. Mencken

"All my good reading, you might say, was done in the toilet. . . . There are passages in *Ulysses* which can be read only in the toilet—if one wants to extract the full flavor of their content."—Henry Miller

"As good almost kill a man as kill a good book: who kills a man kills a reasonable creature, God's image; but he who destroys a good book, kills reason itself, kills the image of God, as it were in the eye."—John Milton

"No entertainment is so cheap as reading, nor any pleasure so lasting."—Lady Mary Wortley Montague

"A book is the only place where you can examine a fragile thought without breaking it, or explore an explosive idea without fear that it will go off in your face."—Edward P. Morgan

"Read every day something no else is reading. Think something no one else is thinking. It is bad for the mind to be always a part of unanimity."—Christopher Morley

"[The pleasures of writing] correspond exactly to the pleasures of reading, the bliss, the felicity of a phrase is shared by writer and reader: by the satisfied writer and the grateful reader, or—which is the same thing—by the artist grateful to the unknown force in his mind that has suggested a combination of images and by the artistic reader whom his combination satisfies."—Vladimir Nabokov

"I find that only by expanding the mind, by reading and talking to people, can you then write anything that makes any sense at all."—Richard Nixon

"As sheer casual reading matter, I still find the English dictionary the most interesting book in our language."—Albert Jay Nock

"Like dreaming, reading performs the prodigious task of carrying us off to other worlds. But reading is not dreaming because books, unlike dreams, are subject to our will: they envelop us in alternative realities only because we give them explicit permission to do so. Books are the dreams we would most like to have, and, like dreams, they have the power to change consciousness, turning sadness to laughter and anxious introspection to the relaxed contemplation of some other time and place."—Victor Null

"Language makes culture, and we make a rotten culture when we abuse words."—Cynthia Ozick

"A book, like a person, has its fortunes with one; is lucky or unlucky in the precise moment of its falling in our way, and often by some happy accident counts with us for something more than its independent value."—Walter Pater

"Books, like friends, should be few and well chosen."—Samuel Paterson

"You make an acquaintance with a book as you do with a person. After ten or fifteen pages, you know with whom you have to deal."—Shimon Peres

"I divide all readers into two classes; those who read to remember and those who read to forget."—William L. Phelps

"If a nation's literature declines, the nation atrophies and decays."—Ezra Pound

"In books I have traveled, not only to other worlds, but into my own. I learned who I was and who I wanted to be, what I might aspire to, and what I might dare to dream about my world and myself."—Anna Quindlen

"Good travel books are novels at heart."—Jonathan Raban

"Reading makes immigrants of us all. It takes us away from home, but, most important, it finds homes for us everywhere."—Hazel Rochman

"Such is the benefit of language: by finding public words to describe ones feelings, one can describe oneself to oneself. One names what was previously only darkly felt."—Richard Rodriguez

"Many voracious readers prefer an evening browsing the bookshelves in their favorite bookstore to an evening socializing with friends. Reading is their form of play; it's their favorite leisure-time activity."—Nadine Rosenthal

[Holden, in *Catcher in the Rye*] "What really knocks me out is a book that, when you're all done reading it, you wish the author that wrote it was a terrific friend of yours and you could call him up on the phone whenever you felt like it."—J. D. Salinger

"There are books in which the footnotes or comments scrawled by some reader's hand in the margin are more interesting than the text."—George Santayana

"All that I know about my life, it seems, I have learned in books."—Jean-Paul Sartre

"Beyond the formative effects of reading on the individuals composing society, the fact that they have read the same books gives them experiences and ideas in common. These constitute a kind of shorthand of ideas which helps make communication quicker and more efficient. That is what we mean when we say figuratively of another person, 'We speak the same language.'"—Charles Scribner Jr.

"Don't ask who's influenced me. A lion is made up of the lambs he's digested, and I've been reading all my life."—Giorgos Seferis

"People get nothing out of books but what they bring to them."—George Bernard Shaw

"Cultivate above all things a taste for reading. There is no pleasure so cheap, so innocent, and so remunerative as the real, hearty pleasure and taste for reading."—Lord Sherbrooke

"We shouldn't teach great books; we should teach a love of reading."—B. F. Skinner

"Let us see the result of good food in a strong body, and the result of great reading in a full and powerful mind."—Sydney Smith

"Reading is to the mind what exercise is to the body."—Sir Richard Steele

"A great book should leave you with many experiences, and slightly exhausted at the end. You live several lives while reading it."—William Styron

"Sometimes I read a book with pleasure, and detest the author."—Johanthan Swift

"One sure window into a person's soul is his reading list."—Mary B. W. Tabor

"She would read anything from a dictionary to a treatise on turnips. Print fascinated her, dazed her, made her good for nothing."—Kylie Tennant

"Read the best books first, or you may not have a chance to read them at all."—Henry David Thoreau

"Education . . . has produced a vast population able to read but unable to distinguish what is worth reading, an easy prey to sensations and cheap appeals."—G. M. Trevelyan

"Books are the carriers of civilization. Without books, history is silent, literature dumb, science crippled, thought and speculation at a standstill."—Barbara Tuchman

"A good book is the best of friends, the same to-day and for ever."—Martin Farquhar Tupper

"A classic is something that everybody wants to have read and nobody wants to read."—Mark Twain

"My family can always tell when I'm well into a novel because the meals get very crummy."—Anne Tyler

"The subjective viewpoint is the only one to use regarding a library. Your true library is a collection of the books you want. You may have deplorably poor taste or bad judgment. Never mind. Correct those traits before you exchange your books."—Carolyn Wells

"A charming British author joined me. She was eloquent and witty and I didn't even have to hold up my end of the conversation. All I had to do was turn pages. Because I had a book, I was not alone."—Carol Weston

"Busy readers are seldom good readers. He who would read with pleasure and profit should have nothing else to do or to think of."—C. M. Wieland

"Thy books should, like thy friends, not many be,/ Yet such wherein men may thy judgment see."—William Wycherley

"People don't realize how a man's whole life can be changed by one book."—Malcolm X

ABOUT THE AUTHOR

Cynthia Lee Katona earned her bachelor's and master's degrees in English and American literature from California State University at Hayward and was voted a Who's Who among America's Teacher in 1998, 2003, and 2004. She is a professor of English, journalism, photography, women's studies, international education, and desktop publishing at Ohlone College. Professor Katona didn't read a book until she was fourteen years old, and has been making up for lost time ever since. When she is not reading or writing, she is on eBay collecting Zuni fetishes, Japanese netsuke, and Chinese inside-painted bottles.